Scandinavian Flint

Scandinavian Flint

– an Archaeological Perspective

Anders Högberg & Deborah Olausson

Aarhus University Press

Langelandsgade 177

DK-8200 Aarhus N

Denmark

Phone +45 8942 5370

Fax +45 8942 5380

www.unipress.dk

Scandinavian Flint

– an Archaeological Perspective

Authors Anders Högberg and Deborah Olausson

Photo of flint samples Merja Vazques Diaz

Graphic design Anders Gutehall

Print Narayana Press

Printed in Denmark 2007

ISBN 978-87-7934-278-1

Preface

This book grew out of our gnawing feeling that, even though we have dealt with Scandinavian flint in a highly practical and pragmatic manner for many years, we still poorly understood this versatile and plentiful material. As archaeologists, our interest lies primarily in looking at how prehistoric people dealt with flint, what they might have seen as the strengths and weaknesses of the various kinds of flint available, how suitable each was for different purposes, where it could have been found, etc. But in order to answer such questions, it is also necessary that we as archaeologists are able to talk to each other about flint in an informed and informative manner. Working with this book has made us appreciate both the complexity and the beauty of Scandinavian flint. We hope that our colleagues will share our enthusiasm and will find the book of use in constructing narratives about the past.

The seminar which launched the project in May 2001 was financed jointly by the Ebbe Kock Fund, the Department of Archaeology and Ancient History in Lund, and Malmö Heritage in Malmö. Funding for the collation and writing of the book was provided by the Swedish Research Council. Funds for chemical sourcing were provided by Birgit och Gad Rausings Stiftelse för Humanistisk Forskning and by Stiftelsen Elisabeth Rausings Minnesfond. Financial support for editing and printing was provided by Malmö Kulturhistoriska Förening, Folke Malmbergs och Birgit Slangerups Fund, Dronning Margrethe II's Arkæologiske Fond, and Crafoordska stiftelsen.

We particularly wish to thank seminar participants for joining in this work and for providing flint samples and published references. We would also like to thank Dr Thomas Terberger of Ernst Moritz Arndt University, Greifswald, and Dr Hilmar Schnick, Nationalparkamt Jasmund, for guiding us on our visit to Rügen and Mikkel Sørensen for guiding us on our trip to Valsømagle, Denmark. We are greatly indebted to Berit Valentin Eriksen, who gave generously of her time and knowledge, first during our visit to northwestern Jutland and later when she read and commented on the contents of the book. Our friend and colleague Arne Sjöström contributed his knowledge and enthusiasm during numerous fieldtrips in search of Kristianstad flint. Thanks also to Stevns Lokalhistoriske Arkiv for their hospitality and for permission to use photographs from their database and to Erik Olausson for graphics. Photography of the flint samples was executed by Merja Vazquez Diaz, Malmö Museum. Graphic design has been competently and creatively carried out by Anders Gutehall, Malmö Heritage.

Table of contents

Scandinavian flint   71

Results and new observations   149

Bibliography   151

Introduction and aims

We must first accept the fact, however, that there are no inherent categories and that there is no consensus even among geologists as to how chert should be subdivided. In other words, a typology of cherts would be as arbitrary as any of the other typologies we deal with; a typology based on mode of origin would subdivide the chert universe differently from one based on visible, chemical, or mechanical properties. Therefore, as with our other typologies, we must start by giving serious thought to the question of how we would want to use such a typology and what we would expect it to do (Luedtke 1992:105).

Flint or chert has been an integrated part of peoples' daily lives in many parts of the globe for the entire prehistoric period. Knowledge about flint, its properties, its uses, and its many names, was no doubt transmitted through the generations as part of everyday life. Just as Smilla, the protagonist in Peter Høeg's novel *Smilla's Sense of Snow* set in Greenland (Høeg 1994), knew more than 100 words for snow and ice, we can assume that the vocabularies of prehistoric people included many and varied terms for what we today call flint.

Those of us who deal with flint today are highly aware of differences in its qualities and properties, but we experience these from our own perspective. In this book we suggest a classification of Scandinavian flint into 17 types, based on our own observations and those of other archaeologists who have studied flint. We make no claim that the categorization we suggest here bears any resemblance to any prehistoric classification. However, it is our hope that this book can be a useful guide for archaeologists working with the prehistoric as well as the historic uses of flint.

For a number of years, archaeologists in the Scandinavian countries have been using Carl Johan Becker's classification of Scandinavian flint types, published in 1952, to describe and classify the varieties of flint used by prehistoric populations (Becker 1952a, 1988). To some extent this system corresponds to the geological classification system, but archaeologists often feel the need for a typology which considers other qualities than those used by geologists, such as a material's workability or its availability to prehistoric populations. Further, Becker's system is not always adequate even for archaeological uses, which has led to the rise of new typologies and terminologies, creating confusion and an increasing lack of consensus.

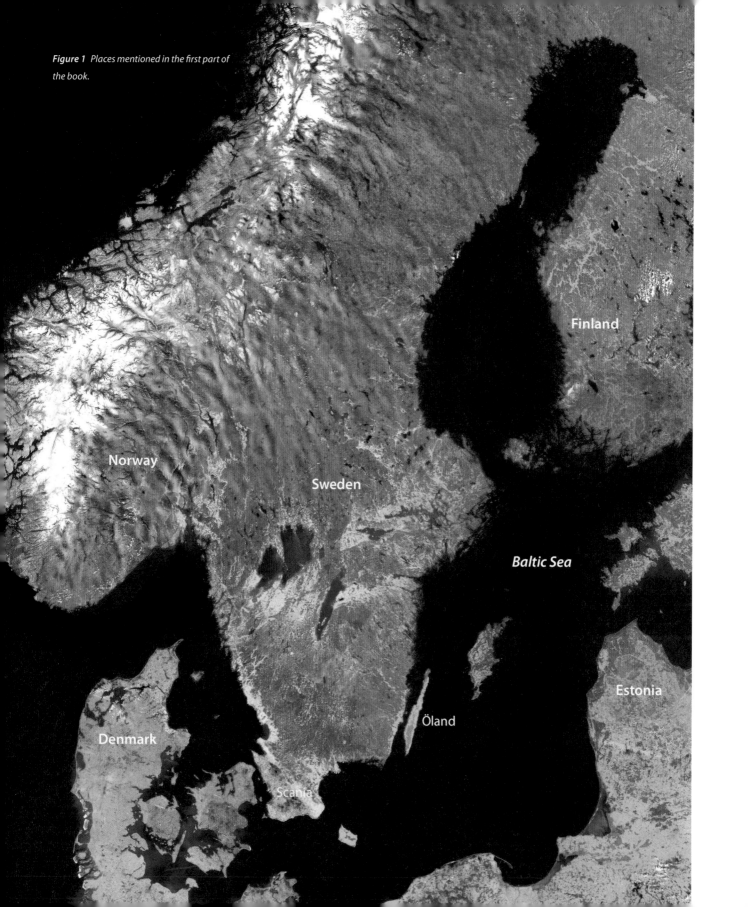

Figure 1 *Places mentioned in the first part of the book.*

Oslo

Jomfruland

Lake Vänern

Fjällbacka

Kinnekulle

Bohuslän

Skagerrak

Kattegat

Västra Hagen

Hillerslev-Hov-Bjerre
Thisted

Aalborg

Varberg

Skovbakken

Halland

Blegvad

Fornæs

Laholm Bay

Djursland

Grönhögen

Sejerø

Scania

Jutland

Copenhagen

Zealand

Funen

Valsømagle

Stevns Klint

Klintholm

Fakse

Rødvig

Møn

Møns Klint

Bornholm

Falster

Hvideklint

Lolland

Hasselø

Jasmund

Rügen

Båstad

Hanaskog

Lake Ivön

Kristianstad

Arup

Glumslöv

Rönneholm

Saxå River

Tågerup

Öresund

Lund

Haväng

Södra Sallerup

Knäbäckshusen

Malmö

Sibbarp/Limhamn

Kämpinge

Mossby

Östra Torp

Figure 1 (Cont.) *Places mentioned in the first part of the book. Detailed map of Scania.*

The major aim of this book is to describe and define Scandinavian flint types, to note what characterizes each type and where it is available, and to establish a uniform terminology. Although some attempts have been made to differentiate between flint sources on the basis of their trace elements (see below), we recognize that most archaeologists will continue to seek a classification system which is based on appearance. Our aim is therefore to illustrate the complexity in the visible properties of Scandinavian flint and to attempt to define flint types on the basis of physical appearance.

> *To be of value to prehistoric peoples the stone must be accessible, free from internal defects, and of sufficient size for reduction. Thus we cannot simply look at a geologic map to determine the distribution of archaeologically significant lithic resources. Geologists simply do not make the necessary distinctions between culturally useful and useless stone* (Church 1994:2).

It is increasingly obvious to archaeologists in Scandinavia that our picture of which flint types were available prehistorically, and our evaluations of their relative attractiveness from a flintknapper's point of view, is much too simple. A further aim of the book is therefore to elucidate what flint types could have been available to prehistoric populations in Scandinavia as raw material and to make some estimation of their qualities in terms of tool-making. We hope that this will provide archaeologists with a natural baseline against which to evaluate prehistoric peoples' choices of raw material in the different contexts in which flint is encountered archaeologically. We evaluate the flint types in terms of practical qualities such as knappability, limitations posed by nodule size, and hypothetical prehistoric availability, rather than in terms of morphogenesis or chemical composition, as geologists do.

For readers who would like to delve more deeply into methods for defining flint types we recommend *Lithic Resource Studies: A Sourcebook for Archaeologists* (1994) by Tim Church or *An Archaeologist's Guide to Chert and Flint* (1992) by Barbara E. Luedtke. Although these books are written from an American rather than a European perspective, the methods and strategies they present are also pertinent for analyzing Scandinavian flint. For those who wish more information about European flint we recommend the comprehensive website FlintSource.net (http://flintsource.net).

Sample collection and flint classification

Sampling methods have been the subject of extensive discussion (Odell 2004). The sample which is the basis for this book is delimited by the archaeologists who contributed to a flint seminar organized by the authors in May 2001. Seminar participants were chosen with the aim of achieving a good geographical representation which would capture the existing variation in flint types from different regions.[1] They were asked to bring raw material samples that they considered typical for all local flint types in their respective areas. Thus, each individual's interest and background; i.e., the materials and regions he or she has been working with, delineate the samples. This implies that the sampling combines knowledge about the lithic materials represented in different archaeological industries with knowledge about lithic resources in Scandinavia. This has made it possible to cover large areas. Follow-up sampling for special cases presented in the text has been carried out by the authors in southern

Figure 2 Participants in the flint seminar, May 2001. From left, back row: Hans Gurstad-Nilsson, Dan Kärre-fors, Lars Larsson, Anders Högberg, Mikkel Sørensen, Kenneth Alexandersson; second row: Jaqueline Taffinder, Jenny Eliasson, Berit Valentin Eriksen, Elisabeth Rudebeck, Bo Knarrström; front row: Arne Sjöström, Deborah Olausson, Bengt Nordquist. Photo by Malmö Museum, Malmö.

Sweden, Denmark, and Rügen in Germany. The information contained in the book thus represents a compilation of the knowledge and experience of the seminar participants, evaluated and assessed in connection with information and descriptions found in published sources.

The seminar yielded a total of 52 flint samples representing all the different flint types known to us from Sweden, Denmark and part of the Baltic Sea coast of northern Germany. Subjective variables such as flint structure and color were discussed at the seminar so that all the samples could be evaluated according to the same criteria. In preparation for the book the authors have carefully studied, described and photographed these samples. We have been able to group the 52 samples together into types, reducing the number of separate types we propose to 17.

Reference collections containing samples of all the types presented here are available for study at Department of Archaeology and Ancient History in Lund, Sweden and at Malmö Heritage in Malmö, Sweden.

Figure 3 Dr Hilmar Schnick and Dr Thomas Terberger on the beach at Rügen, Germany. Unfortunately they were unable to attend the seminar but very kindly shared their knowledge with us during our visit to Rügen.

Scandinavia and the Weichsel glaciation

The term "Scandinavian" in the book's title requires a brief explanation. In this book we have chosen to use the term to refer to the area which covers modern Denmark, Sweden, Norway, and part of the Baltic Sea coast of northern Germany. The topography and physical geography of this area vary a great deal. For example, Denmark

and southern Sweden consist of a fully cultivated landscape with low relief, while in the north the Swedish and Norwegian mountain range rises more than 1,000 meters above sea level. Characteristic for Scandinavia also is its long coastlines consisting of sandy beaches or rocky fjords.

The radical climate shifts during the last 20,000 years have had great impact on the environment in Scandinavia. During warmer periods the ice sheet melted, resulting in glacial meltwater cutting through the landscape, while during colder periods the ice sheet built up, creating increased pressure on the land and transforming the landscape by ice movement.

The main part of the Weichsel glaciation began with an ice advance from the north, and striae on rocks on the west coast of Sweden show that towards the end of the glaciation the area was dominated by an iceflow from the northeast (Påsse 1992:271). At the same time Baltic ice from the east or southeast covered Scania and parts of Denmark. The northern glacier retreated towards the east and northeast while the Baltic ice receded towards the south and southeast. During the deglaciation, a separate iceflow – the Kattegat ice coming from the north – may have existed just west of Bohuslän and northern Halland (Werner 1974:128).

Figure 4 Photograph from the Flint seminar in May 2001. The samples submitted by the participants were displayed on the tables. Flint was knapped and discussed during the course of the day and verbal descriptions of the different samples were compared. Guidelines about what to discuss and how to verbalize characteristics were circulated in advance. No manuals or pre-established definitions were used because the nature of the material makes it almost impossible to standardize the descriptions in advance. As Julie Francis notes: "For example, color is difficult to describe, and my own experience suggests that for any one source area, we can probably use the entire Munsell Soil Color Chart book for descriptions" (Francis 1994:232).

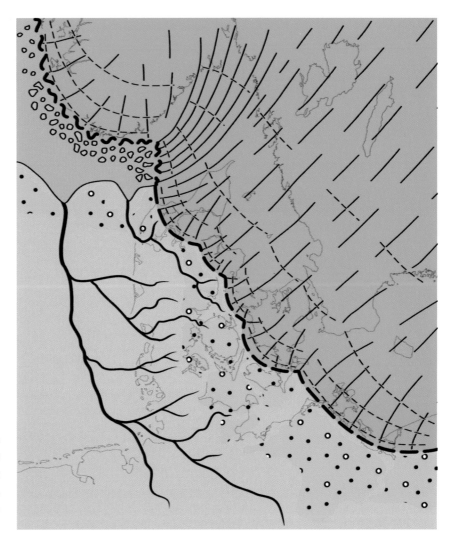

Figure 5 *Paleographical reconstruction during the Last Glacial Maximum sequence at 21,000–19,000 years BP. Key: Dashed line=terrestrial ice margin, light green area=dead-ice, light gray=land, blue=sea, heavy lines=proglacial rivers (from Houmark-Nielsen & Kjær 2003:778, with permission).*

Glacial movement has created a situation where the moraine deposits covering the bedrock contain rocks from many different sources. For example, the till in the north and northwest of Jutland, Denmark contains rocks originating in the Norwegian bedrock, while in the south and southeast it contains rocks from the Swedish bedrock (Gang Rasmussen 1999). Even when the bedrock origin of a specific kind of raw material is known, the large numbers of different raw materials in the till make it almost impossible to point out where the raw material used for any specific tool production was collected originally.

Another effect of the glaciations is the variation in sea level due to ice melt and isostatic uplift. Sea levels rose as ice melted during interstadials, while isostatic uplift caused the land to rise. The fluctuations between these phenomena meant that during the stone age the coastlines in southern Scandinavia were constantly changing. Periodical transgressions and regressions eroded coastal cliffs, creating abundant raw material sources on the beaches and in beach ridges.

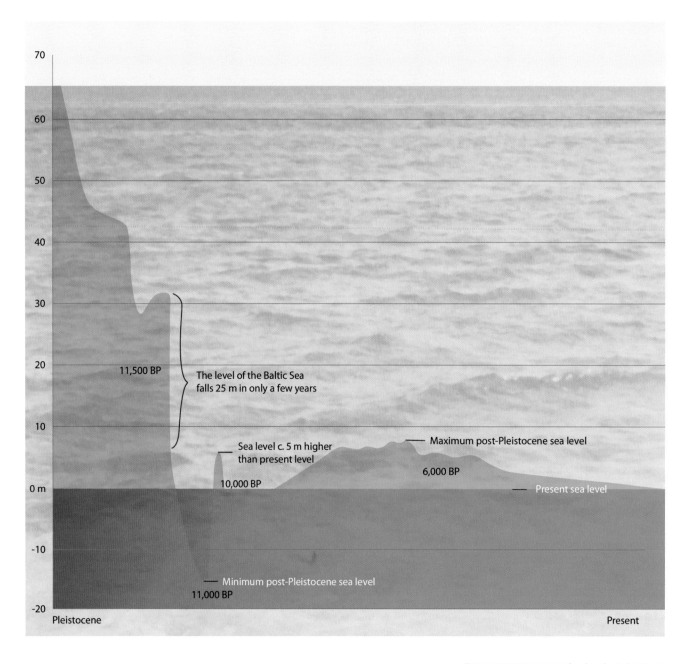

70
60
50
40
30
20 — 11,500 BP
The level of the Baltic Sea
falls 25 m in only a few years
10
Sea level c. 5 m higher
than present level
Maximum post-Pleistocene sea level
6,000 BP
0 m
10,000 BP
Present sea level
-10
Minimum post-Pleistocene sea level
11,000 BP
-20
Pleistocene   Present

Primary and secondary sources

Flint can be found in primary deposits in Denmark and in southern Sweden. No natural deposits of flint exist in the northern part of Sweden and Norway. Geological formations containing flint or its fossil derivates are not found in Finland (Matiskainen, *et al.* 1989:625).

In southern Scandinavia there are numerous outcrops of flint of Danian, Maastrichtian and Campanian age (Högberg, *et al.* 2001). These sources have been

Figure 6 Variation in sea level in the Baltic Sea in eastern Scania from late Pleistocene until the present. Modified from an illustration by Anna Åström, Board of National Antiquities, Lund, Sweden.

Figure 7 *Postglacial transgressions and regressions in southern Scandinavia have eroded coastal moraines made up of sand, clay and rubble. Coastal moraines can contain flint nodules and other rocks suitable for tool production. Erosion exposes rocks on the beaches. Photograph of the beach at Glumslöv, western Scania.*

exploited *in situ* by prehistoric people to a varying extent, either through mining efforts or by taking advantage of flint layers eroding out of cliff faces. Primary sources are augmented by secondary ones located in glacial moraines and on beaches, where ice movements have excavated flint from primary sources and redeposited it, creating a complex "cocktail" of different flint types over large parts of Denmark and southern Sweden (Thomsen 2000). In some parts of southern Scandinavia the chalk or limestone bedrock lies exposed, while in other areas it can be buried under thick layers of moraine.

Figure 8 Flint samples from the beach at Glumslöv, western Scania. Nodules of varying sizes, many of them suitable for production of stone tools, can be found. The nodule in front is c. 20 cm long.

Figure 9 The beach at Kämpinge, southwestern Sweden. Both the beach and beach ridge here are rich in flint. Wind and sand movement continuously alter the appearance of the beach. We know that when Werner (1974) visited this beach some 30 years ago she encountered a sandy beach with only 3 pieces of flint visible (observation point 6, figure 52).

Figure 10 Samples of Matte Danian Flint, Östra Torp Variety collected on the beach at Kämpinge, southwestern Scania. The beach is full of fist-sized flint nodules which have been heavily rounded by the sea. Larger nodules can be found in some areas along the beach. The largest we have encountered, such as the one to the left in the picture, are up to c. 50 cm long.

Distinguishing between primary and secondary sources is important for determining availability and can be a factor for evaluating knappability. This last point has been debated in the archaeological literature for a number of years. The generally accepted position, at least in Scandinavia, is that moraine flint is inferior to flint extracted from a primary source. Some authors attribute inferiority to weaknesses in nodules caused by battering during ice transport and subsequent weathering.

Figure 11 *Modern availability of flint on the beach at Sibbarp near Limhamn in southwestern Scania. Large amounts of both Gray Band Danian Flint and Matte Danian Flint, Östra Torp Variety from a modern limestone quarry have been used here as filling. The nodules are of various sizes and all are high quality flint.*

Figure 12 Archaeologist and knapper Bruce Bradley with Olausson on the beach at Havräng, southeastern Scania. Nodules of Common Kristianstad Flint of various sizes, from fist-sized to c. 15 cm in diameter, are visible on the beach.

Others emphasize that size is the important variable; nodules in the moraine are seldom large, making them unsuitable for large tools (Becker 1952b, 1959; Care 1979; Knarrström 2001). However, Briggs has proposed that in some situations erratic flint can be superior to mined flint. This is because the hard nature of this flint is due to a process of natural selection within the ice. Flawed or cracked nodules are broken down into their smallest indestructible particle thermally and by percussion, ensuring the survival of only the most stable nodules (Briggs 1986:188).

Figure 13 Rocks are constantly eroded out of the beach ridge (line of trees) on the beach at Knäbäckshusen in southeastern Scania. Among these rocks are nodules of Common Kristianstad Flint ranging in size from fist-sized to c. 20 cm. The dynamic forces of storms, wind and streams change the character of this beach from year to year. On some occasions the visitor is met by a sandy beach, on others, a rocky shore.

Figure 14 *An example of difficulties with sampling flint in Scandinavia. The photograph shows flint samples from the beach at Grönhögen on southwestern Öland, collected by Högberg in 1995. The beach pebbles are a flint type which looks like Scandinavian Senonian Flint, but no natural outcrops of this flint exist on Öland. The type of flint which normally can be found here is the Ordovician Flint, which occurs in secondary deposits. The origin of these samples therefore gave us a bit of a headache.*

The answer lies in attempts to establish a brickyard at the beginning of the 20th century. The idea was to extract local schist and produce bricks with burned schist as the main component. The plan was to crush the burned schist in mills, using imported ball flints as crushers. In 1928 the industry was ready to be launched. The burned schist was milled to schist ash. But it appears that most of the ash ended up outside the brickyard. One author reports that 50 years after this happened people were still talking about the giant cloud of dust which spread over the neighborhood (Lundberg 1976:128). Of course the inhabitants were not happy about this and the brickyard had to shut down after only one day in operation. The ball flint intended for use as crushers in the mill was dumped into the sea. Almost 80 years afterwards, the ball flint ended up as a sample in our collection. The nodules are c. 5 cm long.

Our experience tells us that the situation is complicated. There is no necessary relationship between flint quality and origin in primary vs. secondary sources (Luedtke 1992:82). Flint from primary sources can be of good or bad quality, as can flint from secondary sources. For example, at Järavallen at Sibbarp in southwestern Scania, deposits of large, good quality moraine flint nodules were exploited for axe manufacture during the Neolithic (figure 15) (Högberg 2002; Kjellmark 1905). About twenty similar sites are known in Denmark (Ebbesen 1980; Kempfner-Jørgensen & Liversage 1985).

All of the samples we have used for classification have been collected by archaeologists but they are geological specimens; i.e., the flint samples are not archaeological artifacts but rather unworked rocks collected from different outcrops or in secondary deposits. Because patination and weathering processes can radically alter flint's appearance (see the chapter Weathering and patination below), considerable effort was made to obtain pristine flint samples from primary sources.

Three of the 17 types, namely Ordovician Flint, West Swedish Beach Flint, and Ball Flint, are exceptional in that these types contain flint which has been transported by ice movement and deposited on beaches rather than originating in a primary deposit. Therefore the type may include flint of different origins and ages. We have chosen to identify these as archaeological types with the motivation that they have been exploited as primary sources of raw material during prehistory.

Figure 15 Flint tool preforms from a beach ridge at Sibbarp on the west coast of Scania. The find consists mainly of preforms for square-sectioned and point-butted axes, chisels and bifaces. The majority are of various types of flint of Danian age, while a few are Scandinavian Senonian Flint. The preform to the lower left is c. 15 cm long. Photo by Merja Vazquez Diaz, Malmö Museum, Malmö.

Scandinavian Flint

Flint in general and Scandinavian flint in particular

What is flint?

The terms "flint" and "chert" are often used interchangeably and there is a lack of consensus among archaeologists as to what to call fine-grained, knappable siliceous rocks. Some regard flint as a type of chert while others consider flint to be one type of rock and chert another (Luedtke 1992). North American and British archaeologists differentiate between "chert" and "flint", while in general Scandinavian archaeologists refer only to flint; in fact there is no word for "chert" in any of the Scandinavian languages.

According to the geological definition, chert is a classificatory term for chemically precipitated, very pure, siliceous sedimentary rock. It is composed of opal, chalcedony and quartz with a few accessory minerals and occasional organic residues (Kinnunen, *et al.* 1985:20–21). Cherts can occur as nodules or as bedded deposits. Geologists define flint as the nodular variety of chert occurring typically in the Cretaceous chalk deposits of southern England and western Europe. The chemical structure of flint and chert is the same; the difference between them is only a matter of grain size, porosity, and dehydration features (Thurston 1978:119–120). Both are microcrystalline (Thomsen 2000:25) and their excellent mechanical properties can be explained by their microstructure, which consists of a network of quartz crystallites with numerous pores filled with water (Kinnunen, *et al.* 1985:21).

In this book we will follow the Scandinavian practice and refer to all chert varieties as flint.

Flint formation

European Cretaceous flints formed under unusual conditions compared with most other flints and cherts. During the Late Cretaceous Period, sea levels were especially high all over the world. Many low-lying continental areas, including much of England and northern Europe, were inundated by shallow seas 150 to 200 m deep. Very little sediment from land washed into the seas. Consequently, deposits on the continental shelves consist almost entirely of the calcareous shells of silica-rich organisms. The well-oxygenated floor of this Late Cretaceous sea provided perfect conditions for a variety of organisms that mixed and churned the soft, limey muds. Such organisms excavated burrows in the semi-consolidated chalk and these filled gradually with

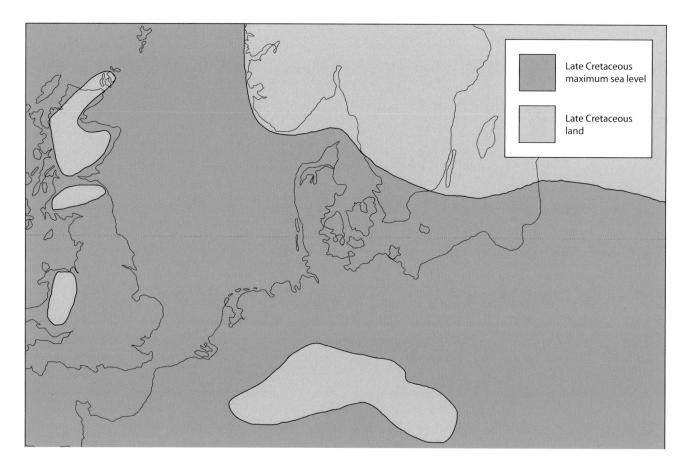

soft, porous sediments and attracted algae, fungi, worms and other organisms. Flint formation started in these burrows (Luedtke 1992; McDonnell, *et al.* 1997; Surlyk & Håkansson 1999).

Flint is formed in chalk or limestone sediments in a process known as diagenesis. Diagenesis refers to all the physical, chemical, and biological changes that a sediment undergoes after the grains are deposited and while it is becoming a rock, but before it is metamorphosed or weathered (Luedtke 1992:139). Flint consists of almost pure silica dioxide (SiO_2) which can occur in the form of opal or chalcedony. It is a chemical sediment; that is, silica must go into solution in water and then be precipitated out again in order for flint to form (Luedtke 1992:18). It is formed as calcite or calcium carbonate is dissolved and replaced by silica which comes from organisms such as sponges, diatoms, or radiolaria (Odell 2004:20; Schmid 1986:3; Thomsen 2000:22). Flint occurs as beds or in nodules, depending on the volume of silica available for silicification (Thurston 1978:121). When a flint nodule is formed by diagenesis in a bed of limestone or chalk, the center will usually contain a fragment of fossil organic material. Around this core, microcrystals of silica form concentrically if the silica-charged waters continue to permeate the deposit of chalk or limestone. Most of the non-carbonate minerals found in the chalk sediments are preserved *in situ* in the new matrix of flint (Craddock, *et al.* 1983:138).

Figure 16 Palaeogeography of northern Europe at the time of the Cretaceous/Tertiary boundary (redrawn from Håkansson & Thomsen 1999:68, with permission).

Scandinavian Flint

Figure 17 *The chalk cliffs at Møns Klint, Denmark.*

Flint formation can involve more than one episode of silicification, thousands or even millions of years apart. Some concentrically banded nodules may have formed in several stages of silicification. Flints commonly contain small cracks or cavities that were filled with chalcedony or macrocrystalline quartz crystals long after the bulk of the flint formed (Luedtke 1992:27). A change in color resulting from different amounts of absorbed mineral salts or a different mineral being taken into solution by silica-charged waters can occur (Crabtree 1967:15). The colors and textures exhibited by flints are determined by impurities and by the texture of the parent rock (Thomsen 2000; Thurston 1978). Many flints contain patches of their host rock (i.e. chalk or limestone) and some of them are surrounded by a grayish-white transitional zone testifying to their incomplete silicification (Kinnunen, *et al.* 1985:22).

Figure 18 *Flint layers in a vertical position in chalk cliffs at Møns Klint, Denmark. The stratigraphy here has been rearranged by thrust-faulting in a Late Weichselian ice advance and subsequently superimposed by thrust-faulting from the east during the very latest Weichselian ice advance reaching Denmark (Surlyk & Håkansson 1999:55).*

Flint in southern Scandinavia, locations and geology

Literally millions of flint artifacts from prehistoric contexts in Scandinavia are known. Axes, daggers, chisels, blades, knives, scrapers, drills, burins, and projectile points are examples of tools made from flint. The vast majority of the flint types occurring in Scandinavia were formed during the Late Cretaceous and Early Tertiary periods. Archaeologists working in southern Scandinavia generally distinguish among Danian, Senonian, or Kristianstad flint.

Period	Epoch	Age	Geologic time M.Y.
			0,01
Neogene	Holocene		
	Pleistocene		
	Pliocene		
	Miocene		
			23,0
Paleogene	Oligocene		
	Eocene		
	Paleocene	Danian	
			65,5
Cretaceous	Senonian	Maastrichtian	
		Campanian	
			145,5
Jurassic			
			199,6
Triassic			
			251,0
Permian			
			299,0
Carboniferous			
			359,2
Devonian			
			416,0
Silurian			
			443,7
Ordovician			
			488,3
Cambrian			

Figure 19 Geological time scale, showing the position of the Senonian epoch, the Danian, Maastrichtian and Campanian ages, and the Cretaceous, Cambrian, and Ordovician periods.

Small amounts of more than 400 million-year-old flint from the Ordovician Period also occur on the Baltic Sea floor. This flint was available to prehistoric people as secondary deposits on beaches and beach ridges on the Swedish east coast islands of Öland and Gotland (Thomsen 2000). Finally, flint from the Upper Cambrian Period can be found at Kinnekulle in western Sweden (Thomsen 2000:17).

Scania, Sweden

Southern Scandinavia and Denmark lie in the geological formation called the North Sea basin, which covers an area of southern Sweden, northern Germany, Holland, and eastern England (figure 16). Senonian and Danian sediments lie at a depth of 3 km in the center of this basin, but in some areas uplift has raised these to the present surface. Danian limestone containing flint lies at or very near the surface in a band from northern Jutland across northern Zealand and southwestern Scania. Cretaceous chalk containing flint underlies the south Baltic, northern Germany and the Skagerrack and Kattegat Seas, and continues westwards to Holland and southeastern England. Cretaceous layers can be found at or near the surface in the Kristianstad area and in limited spots in southern and northeastern Scania, in southern Zealand, on the islands of Møn, Falster, and Lolland, and on the northern tip of Jutland (Johansen 1987:4; Thomsen 2000:18–21).

Archaeological term	Geological age
Danian flint	Danian age
Senonian flint	Maastrichtian age
Kristianstad flint	Campanian age

Figure 20 The relationship between the use of the archaeological and geological terms when referring to flint in Scandinavian publications.

Figure 21 A cache of two Early Neolithic flint axes found in southern Sweden. Both are made from a high quality Scandinavian Senonian Flint. Patination has altered the color. The axe to the right is 40 cm long. Photo by John Webb, Malmö Museum, Malmö.

As mentioned above, glacial action has rearranged sediments and deposited flint nodules in the glacial tills of Scania, making them quite rich in secondary flint. Transgressions and regressions plus yearly seasonal changes have eroded coastlines, exposing and re-depositing flint nodules. Since sediments with Campanian, Maastrichtian and Danian flints occur in Scania or its immediate surroundings, it is not surprising to note that the soils and beaches of Scania contain examples of all types of flint from all these periods. For example, the northeastern till has rocks originating locally, including Kristianstad flint. Glacial action has also deposited chalk and flint from the Baltic Sea floor on beaches, including ball flint. Ball flint occurs on the east coast and in the eastern moraines in Scania (Tralau 1974:247).

Rocks in the southeastern moraines were deposited by glaciofluvial currents originating from the Baltic Sea. The most common rocks besides those from the bedrock are nodules of light gray matte flint and limestones from the Baltic Sea and from the east and south. Kristianstad flint and Ball flints occasionally occur in southern moraines (Ekström 1936).

Tills in northwestern Scania were deposited by glaciers originating from the northeast (Påsse 1992:271). They contain chalk flint and Danian flint, as well as some Ball flints. Knarrström reports that Kristianstad flint occurs in scattered nodules in the till of northwestern Scania (Knarrström 1997). It is possible that this flint originates from the bedrock here.

At Södra Sallerup in southwestern Scania, enormous slabs of chalk were deposited by glacial ice. These slabs are rich in Senonian flint, which was mined in prehistory (see below).

Figure 22 Geological map showing areas with chalk and limestone bedrock (from Becker 1988 and Vang Petersen 1993). This type of distribution map is often used to illustrate the occurrence of flint. However, this picture is only partially correct. Flint does occur widely in the areas marked on the map, but the amount of flint in each geological formation can vary considerably in each area. For instance, the amount of flint in the limestone deposits in the area around Kristianstad is highly variable. This variability is related to the type of limestone. Limestone containing flint occurs mostly north of Kristianstad (Magnusson, et al. 1963). Key: Hatching diagonally from top left to bottom right = danian layers, hatching diagonally from top right to bottom left = senonian layers, cross-hatching = occurrence of Kristianstad flint.

The Swedish west coast and Norway's southern coast

Erratic Cretaceous and Danian flints occur along the entire Swedish west coast and also along the Norwegian coast (Lidmar-Bergström 1982:98). The origin of these, and the means by which they were transported, is a matter of some debate among geologists. Werner proposes a postglacial introduction of the flint into the area by beach transport or by drift ice from the floor of the Kattegat and Skagerrack Seas or from western Scania and eastern Denmark (Magnusson, *et al.* 1963:300; Werner 1967:239, 1974:123–124). Påsse reports on a qualitative analysis which revealed that the predominant rock types along the west coast are flint and limestone, most of which seem to be of Danian age. On the basis of this, Påsse maintains that the most likely provenience was the Öresund area and that the transport mechanism was glacially derived icebergs drifting northwards to Halland and Bohuslän (Påsse 1992:273, 277, 2004). Lidmar-Bergström (1982:48), however, is of the opinion that some of the flint present in southern Halland is local and derives from former Cretaceous deposits. Rocks of Cretaceous age crop out in the Båstad area and in central Halland (Påsse 1992:271).

Figure 23 A beach at Lake Ivön in northeastern Scania. Nodules of poor quality Common Kristianstad Flint are present here (figure 24).

It seems probable that the entire Halland coast has had or still has outliers of Upper Cretaceous limestone. Where this is dissolved there may still be concentrations of residual flints (Lidmar-Bergström 1982:123). Nodules of flint resembling Kristianstad flint can be found in southern Halland (Knarrström 2000a:16; Lidmar-Bergström 1982:35).

In a field campaign of systematic collection along the Swedish west coast during the 1960s, Werner found that the concentrations of flint were highest between Varberg and Fjällbacka (Werner 1967:234). Lidmar-Bergström (1982:107) reports that the content of flint along the Swedish west coast never exceeds ten per cent, to be compared with the Danish coasts where many beaches show amounts of twenty-five to fifty per cent flint (Påsse 1992:274). Flint in western Sweden north of Scania is limited to the coast, and Werner has noted that flint nodules are extremely rare more than 10 to 15 km inland from the present coastline (Werner 1967:236, 1974:89).

The Norwegian archaeologist Erling Johansen carried out a campaign in the 1950s to survey the amounts and types of flint erratics along Norway's southern coast. He quantified and classified flint nodules on the beaches and up to the highest coastline at 30 m above sea level in an area from the Swedish province of Bohuslän

Figure 24 Samples of Common Kristianstad Flint collected on the beach at Lake Ivön. This flint is of very poor quality, consisting of nodules with a pumice-like texture with small pockets of flint in the center. The "pumice stone" flakes conchoidally and yields fragile cutting edges. This type of flint has been reported in artifacts from Neolithic contexts from a site in northeastern Scania (Knarrström 2007). The largest nodule in the picture is c. 25 cm.

Figure 25 In 1944 the Swedish archaeologist Åke Fredsjö excavated a Mesolithic site in northern Halland called Västra Hagen. The site was discovered during gravel quarrying operations. Fredsjö reports that the excavated cultural layer contained a large number of fist-sized flint nodules, which according to him were "undoubtedly moraine flints" (Fredsjö 1953:105). During the summer of 2005 Högberg examined this assemblage at the museum in Gothenburg. He concluded that Västra Hagen is a former production site located at the raw material source, a beach ridge rich in West Swedish Beach Flint. Fredsjö's photograph shows this beach ridge under excavation. Nodules of West Swedish Beach Flint are visible in the profile. Photo from Göteborgs Stadsmuseum, archives.

and around the Oslo Fjord up to Jomfruland in Norway. He found that flint made up one half to two per cent – in some places up to six per cent – of all the rocks here. Johansen recorded the size of the nodules and found many which were fist-sized or larger. Danian flint and Senonian flint were present, but he found no evidence of Kristianstad flint. Johansen hypothesized that the nodules were transported from Danish and Swedish sources, either by glacial movement or in the postglacial period by sea ice. He concluded that flint suitable for making smaller tools such as scrapers and projectile points was readily available to prehistoric populations. His observations of larger nodules led him to conclude that some of the more elaborate flint tools found in Norway, such as axes, could also have been made from flint collected locally (Johansen 1956). However, in a recent study of polished Neolithic axes from southern Norway, Axel Mjærum states that even if it is possible that some of the axes found in Norway have been made of raw material found on the Norwegian coast, the majority of axes from the area are not made of local flint (Mjærum 2004).

Kinnekulle, Sweden and the Baltic islands of Öland, Gotland and Bornholm

Flint of Campanian, Maastrichtian, or Danian age occurs in primary deposits in Scandinavia only in southernmost Sweden and in Denmark. However, there are limestone layers of much greater age underlying parts of the Baltic Sea and in a few other spots in Sweden, and some of these contain flint. At Kinnekulle, on the southern shore of Lake Vänern in Sweden, a coarse material known as Kinnekulle Flint can be found in alum shale deposits. It occurs as nodules up to 30 cm in diameter but seldom as slabs (Johansson, *et al.* 1943:38). Uplifting has made outcrops of Kinnekulle Flint available to prehistoric populations. The geological age of this flint is generally considered to be Upper Cambrian (Kindgren 1991; Kinnunen, *et al.* 1985; Königsson 1973; Laufeld 1971; Werner 1974).

A broad band of Cambro-Silurian limestone containing flint underlies the Baltic Sea in a curve trending from Estonia towards the southwest and passing Gotland and Öland (Laufeld 1971:96). Nodules and knapped objects of this flint found on Gotland contain fossils which enable geologists to date the flint to the Middle or Upper Ordovician (Kinnunen, *et al.* 1985:35; Laufeld 1971:98; Tralau 1974:247). Nodules are relatively small, seldom larger than 15 cm in diameter, they are often rounded and have a limestone cortex (Königsson 1973; Laufeld 1971; Thorsberg 1997; Tralau 1974; Werner 1974).

There are no known primary deposits of flint to be found in the Cretaceous deposits on Bornholm. However, till deposits contain flint nodules which could be used by prehistoric knappers. Becker (Becker 1952b) distinguishes four types of flint available in the till here: ball flint, Kristianstad flint, and two types of flint of Danian age. In a recent survey whose aim was to inventory the raw material available along the coast, Michael S. Thorsen reported finding several nodules of Senonian flint also (Nielsen 2001; Thorsen 2003; Vang Petersen 2001).

The Danish islands of Zealand, Møn and Lolland-Falster

Sediments containing flint of both Late Maastrichtian and Danian age occur in the cliffs of Stevns Klint on eastern Zealand. Maastrichtian chalk layers contain flint layers 5 to 20 cm thick and 1 to 1.5 vertical meters apart. Flint bands in the Danian limestone layers are 20 to 30 cm thick and c. 1 meter apart. Flint makes up five per cent of the chalk formation and up to twenty per cent of the Danian limestone formation here. Erosion by the sea continuously eats away the chalk layers, and the

Figure 26 Stevns Klint on Zealand, eastern Denmark. Flint of Danian age (upper layers) as well as of Senonian age (lower layers) is present here. Note the clear demarcation between the yellowish limestone and the white chalk. This marks the end of the Cretaceous Period.

Figure 27a Photograph showing Danian flint in situ at Stevns Klint.

Scandinavian Flint

Figure 27b Photograph showing Senonian flint in situ *at Stevns Klint.*

Figure 28 Högberg collecting flint samples at Stevns Klint for chemical analysis.

beach at Stevns is covered with slabs and nodules of flint (Callahan 1980; Floris 1971:16; Gry & Søndergaard 1958:8–9; Thomsen 2000:29–31; Werner 1974:13).

The chalk cliffs at Møns Klint on the island of Møn are of Lower Maastrichtian age. Flint occurs in layers 5 to 10 cm thick and 1 to 1.5 vertical meters apart. Flint nodules are generally small and they make up more than ninety-nine per cent of the rocks on the beach here (Gry & Søndergaard 1958a:8–9; Thomsen 2000:28; Werner 1974:13, 75).

Stevns Klint - Stenbrudet

Figure 29 Limestone quarrying in the Danian layers at Stevns Klint at the beginning of the 20th century. Limestone from Stevns has been an important building material since Absalon used it in the construction of a harbor at Havn, present-day Copenhagen, in 1167. Quarrying at Stevns Klint finally ceased after the Second World War (Wienberg Rasmussen 1984:148). Published by permission from Stevns Lokalhistoriske Arkiv.

Figure 30 Traces of the limestone quarrying are still visible in the cliff at Stevns Klint.

Flint is present in the bryozoan limestone layers of Danian age at Fakse,[2] Zealand (Floris 1992). The Fakse hill is an erosional feature sculpted by the advancing Quaternay ice sheets, which left the broad top of the hill essentially bare of glacigenic cover (Surlyk & Håkansson 1999:47). Glaciations passed over this area several times, excavating Danian limestone and flint and depositing these materials in moraines on the surface (Krüger 1971).

Figure 31 *Olausson on the beach beneath the chalk cliffs at Møns Klint, Denmark preparing flint samples for chemical analysis.*

Geological conditions here are similar to those of western Scania in regard to secondary sources. Limestone and chalk sediments in the neighborhood have contributed flint nodules to the tills and coastlines. Ice rafting and glacial action have transported flint nodules of Danian and Maastrichtian age from their primary sources in large numbers, mixing them up and re-depositing them. In a study of the contents of Danish tills, Wienberg Rasmussen found that twenty to sixty per cent

of the rocks are flint (Gry & Søndergaard 1958; Thomsen 2000; Wienberg Rasmussen 1970). Even isolated nodules of Kristianstad flint, presumably ice transported, can be found on Zealand (Knarrström 1997:9). Becker writes that Zealand flint types can be found in moraines over most of Denmark (Becker 1993:126). Eastern Zealand, Lolland-Falster and northern Jutland have made up one of the world's largest resource areas for flint during prehistoric times (Madsen 1993:126). This is particularly evident on Lolland-Falster, where nodules of high quality Falster Flint dominate clearance cairns and stone walls (see figure 45).

Figure 32 South of the famous cliffs on Møns Klint a small beach cliff, Hvideklint, stretches a few kilometers along the coast. Here the lower layers of the Maastrichtian chalk are older than those at Møns Klint. The geologically oldest Scandinavian Senonian Flint can be found at Hvideklint. The color, form, matrix, and cortex of this flint looks exactly like the other samples of Scandinavian Senonian Flint. However, there is one problem with this flint: it has a white band, similar to that on Gray Band Danian Flint, at the transition between the cortex and the flint. So, even though this flint is a Senonian flint, it has an attribute which is characteristic of some types of Danian flint. This flint is rare, and because in most attributes it is recognizably a Scandinavian Senonian Flint, we have chosen not to define it as a separate type. When this band is present it may be impossible to differentiate single flakes of Hvideklint Scandinavian Senonian Flint from Gray Band Danian Flint (cf. figure 38.).

Figure 33 The stratigraphy at Hvideklint on Møn is a complicated mixture of Lower Maastrichtian chalk containing flint, moraine layers from the Saale glaciation, glacio-fluvial deposits from the Eem interstadial, and sedimentation from the post-glacial period (Surlyk & Håkansson 1999).

Figure 34 *The modern limestone quarry at Fakse, Denmark. Large nodules of Brown Bryozoan Flint can be found here.*

Funen, Denmark

On eastern Funen, near Klintholm, bryozoan limestone of Danian age containing flint lies close to the surface. This flint has a distinctive appearance and according to Thomsen it is the only kind of Scandinavian flint which can be provenienced with certainty on the basis of its appearance (Thomsen 2000; Vang Petersen 1993).

Jutland, Denmark

The situation for Jutland regarding flint is very complex, particularly in the Thisted structure in the north. In a broad band from northern Jutland, across northern Zealand, Scania, and northern Germany, the Danian limestone lies at or close to the surface. At Thisted a salt dome has pressed the Cretaceous and Danian layers

Figure 35 *A thin-butted axe made of flint from the island of Falster. Note how skillfully the Neolithic flintknapper has knapped the edge curvature in line with the curved color patterns in the banded flint. The axe is c. 30 cm long. Photo by Christer Åhlin, the Museum of National Antiquities, Stockholm.*

Figure 36 Högberg gathering flint samples at the quarry at Klintholm, Denmark.

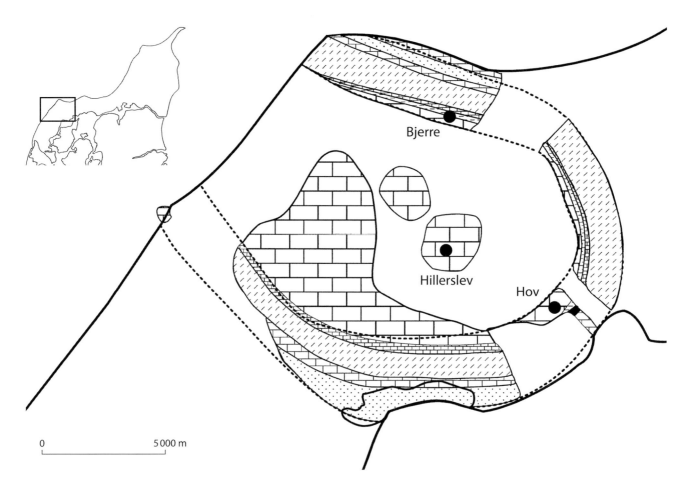

0   5 000 m

upwards into a dome-shaped structure. Glacial action then shaved off the uplifted layers and spread the flint in the surrounding area (Nielsen 1993:48–49). Following the Weichsel glaciation, several transgressions affected the Thisted area and during the Early Neolithic the area was an archipelago, with steep cliffs containing layers of accessible primary and secondary flint (Thomsen 2000).

The Late Maastrichtian chalk at Aalborg is much poorer in flint than contemporary layers at Stevns or Møn (Becker 1993:124; Gry & Søndergaard 1958:8–9). All of the Danish flint types, with the exception of Coarse Bryozoan Flint from Funen, have been easily available here, either as outcrops or in the moraines (Thomsen 2000:35). According to Madsen it is even possible to find nodules of Kristianstad flint in the till at Djursland in northeastern Jutland (Madsen 1993:126). However, Becker writes that secondary sources of flint are less numerous in northern Jutland than what we see in southeastern Denmark and on the Scanian west coast (Becker 1993:121).

In western and central Jutland, glacial activity during the Saale and Weichsel glaciations has deposited flint in moraines, mostly in sizes ranging from sandgrains to pebbles. Nodules large enough for axe manufacture are extremely rare (Nielsen 1997:262).

Figure 37 *The geology of the Thisted structure is complicated. Cretaceous and Danian layers have been pressed upwards in a dome-shaped structure and then eroded, resulting in a mix of different types of flint available at the surface. Large rectangles mark Maastrichtian chalk while areas marked with dots, dashes and medium and small rectangles indicate varities of Danian limestone. The flint mine areas at Bjerre, Hillerslev, and Hov have been marked. Redrawn from Thomsen (2000), with permission.*

Figure 38 *The quarry at Hillerslev, Jutland, Denmark. In this area the salt dome has pressed up the Maastrichtian chalk to the surface. In 1966 Becker excavated prehistoric flint mines here (Becker 1980b). Nodules of Scandinavian Senonian Flint are visible on the surface. A phenomenon similar to what we discovered at Hvideklint on Møn was evident here as well; namely that while the flint itself showed characteristics typical for Scandinavian Senonian Flint, on some nodules a lighter band of flint could be seen just under the cortex. When this band is present, there is a risk that flint from Hillerslev can be confused with Gray Band Danian Flint (cf. figure 32).*

Figure 39 The chalk cliffs at Jasmund in Rügen, Germany.

Figure 40 Flint layers in chalk cliffs at Jasmund in Rügen, Germany.

Scandinavian Flint

Rügen, Germany

Lower to Upper Maastrichtian layers from the northern tip of Jutland continue to southern Zealand, Rügen, and northern Germany. The white chalk cliffs at Jasmund on northeastern Rügen date to the Lower Maastrichtian and as many as 66 flint layers are visible here (Herrig 1995; Werner 1967:229). A characteristic nodule form which can be found at Jasmund are the so called "flowerpots", a term which derives from the modern use of these nodules as garden flowerpots. These nodules are up to one meter in size.

Prehistoric flint mining and flint extraction

There are two main areas in Denmark, both located in northern Jutland, where flint was mined during the Neolithic. To the northeast is the Aalborg area with the Skovbakken site (Becker 1980c) and Blegvad west of Djursland (Madsen 1994), and to the northwest is the Hillerslev–Hov–Bjerre area (Becker 1980a, 1980b).

Prehistoric workshops located on or near beaches and cliffs where good quality flint was abundant have also been identified. At Hastrup Vænget near Stevns Klint in Denmark, debitage from the manufacture of Early Neolithic thin-butted flint axes has been found (Vemming Hansen & Madsen 1983). In the Late Neolithic, flintknapping on a large scale was carried out at Fornæs on Jutland (Glob 1951) and on the island of Sejerø north of Zealand (Kempfner-Jørgensen & Liversage 1985).

Figure 41 *Very large nodules of Rügen Flint can be found on the beach at Jasmund in Rügen, Germany. Some of these contain large concavities and are referred to by local people as "flowerpots". The boot belongs to Högberg, size 42 (EUR) or 8 (UK).*

Figure 42 *The beach at Fornæs with the Sangstrup Klint in the background. At Fornæs the beach and the beach ridges are rich in flint. In 1950 a prehistoric knapping site dated to the Late Neolithic was excavated here (Glob 1951).*

In the area around Södra Sallerup in southwestern Sweden, systematic mining of flint started in the Early Neolithic. This flint is of Maastrichtian age and it occurs embedded in enormous slabs of chalk which were scooped up by glacial ice and re-deposited here (Rudebeck 1987; Rudebeck, *et al.* 1980).

Figure 43 *Aerial view of the Södra Sallerup area in southwestern Scania during topsoil removal for documentation. Prehistoric flint extraction pits are visible as white spots. This is the only known prehistoric flint mining area in Sweden. It is estimated that an area of about 325,000 square meters has been quarried for chalk since the late nineteenth century. Most of this was done without any archaeological documentation. Since the modern chalk quarries were located where the chalk was close to the surface, it is clear that they were simultaneously located in the areas where the prehistoric flint mining was the most intense. Hence, from a surface area of c. 200,000 square meters we have little or no knowledge of the prehistoric activities. However we do have documentation of varying quality from c. 125,000 square meters. In the 1980s this area with about 400 flint mineshafts and pits was declared a National Heritage Monument and protected from future exploitation by the Board of National Antiquities (from Högberg, et al. 2001).*

At three sites in the beach ridges along the western and southwestern coast of Sweden, large numbers of preforms for Neolithic axes and daggers have been found (see figure 15) indicating that the outcrops there were "mined" during prehistory (Hansen 1929; Högberg 2002).

In systematic field studies to locate primary and secondary flint deposits, the authors have found two further flint outcrop sites which may have been accessible to prehistoric populations. The first of these is at Östra Torp on the southern coast of Scania. Here, and in a few other places to the west along the coast, we discovered outcrops of Danian flint exposed on the beach. This is to our knowledge the only area in southern Sweden where flint in bedrock is visible on the surface. The second site is at Hanaskog in northeastern Scania. Högberg discovered large quantities of Kristianstad flint debitage from the manufacture of large blade knives in the Late Bronze Age in the fields near the modern limestone quarry (Högberg 2005). This indicates that deposits of Kristianstad flint must have been accessible when such knives were being manufactured.

Figure 44 *Högberg at the newly discovered outcrop of flint on the beach at Östra Torp, southern Sweden.*

Availability

Walking in ploughed fields in southwestern Scania or many parts of Denmark today, one is often struck by the amount of flint lying in the furrows. According to Gry & Søndergaard (1958:5) between ten and fifty per cent of the rocks in the Danish till are flint. On the former island of Hasselø, west of Falster, heaps of large nodules of fine quality Falster Flint have been piled up by farmers anxious to be rid of these impediments to modern ploughing. Rolled and rounded flint nodules are common along the coasts of Denmark and the west coast of Sweden.

However, Knarrström cautions against viewing the present-day situation in ploughed fields as a reflection of the prehistoric world. Many source-critical processes work to distort the picture of prehistoric flint availability in moraine deposits. For instance, farmers remove larger rocks to facilitate ploughing. We must also assume that humans have picked up flint since the stone age in order to use it for tools (Knarrström 2000a:111). Such processes mean that there will be less flint available today than in the past. But, ploughing and frost-heaving continuously bring new nodules to the surface in ploughed fields (Knarrström 2000b:104), thus working in the opposite direction and contributing to an increase in the number of nodules today as compared to the past.

Figure 45 Högberg collecting flint on a clearance cairn consisting almost entirely of large nodules of Falster Flint on Falster-Hasselø, Denmark.

	No. of potential flake cores, large	No. of potential flake cores, small	No. of potential scrapers or retouched edges	Total amount of flint, kilograms
Square 1	2	13	14	1.4
Square 2	6	7	12	2.1

Figure 46 *Results from the survey carried out by Högberg (2001:31).*

Högberg carried out an investigation to determine how much of the flint in the moraine could be useful for tool production. He collected all flint available in the ploughzone from two squares 50 × 50 cm on a site south of Malmö. This resulted in 3.5 kg flint, varying in size from nodules 10 × 5 × 4 cm down to small pieces of 1 to 2 cm. Most of the flint was unsuitable for tools because of thick cortex, small size, coarse structure, or high fossil content. But he also found a number of nodules and frost-split pieces which could be used for tools (figure 46).

Conversely, humans have also presumably introduced flint to fields. Lidmar-Bergström observed that flint can be dumped on fields in connection with the use of limestone as agricultural fertilizer (Lidmar-Bergström 1982:102). The lowest quality lime mined at the Faxe quarry in Denmark is used for fertilizing fields. This quality contains one and a half per cent flint or more (Rasmussen & Niss 2002:29).

Another factor we must bear in mind when we try to envision the Mesolithic or Neolithic situation is that most of the landscape was covered by vegetation. In such a landscape, there are very few opportunities to see what lies beneath the surface. Even rocks lying on the surface may be covered by vegetation and thus not visible (Randver 2004).

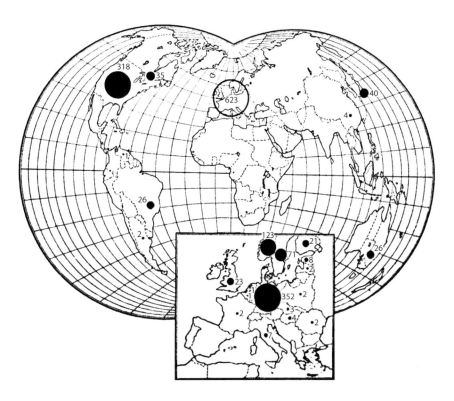

Figure 47 *Map showing the export of "Kugelflint" (Ball Flint) from Stevns Klint in eastern Zealand, Denmark during the years 1936–1938. Over this period the total amount of flint exported was 10,780 tons. This huge industry has scattered Scandinavian flint all over the world. Numbers on the map indicate 10 tons. Published by permission from Stevns Lokalhistoriske Arkiv.*

Figure 48 The harbour in Rødvig south of Stevns Klint in eastern Zealand, Denmark in the beginning of the 20th century. Huge piles of flint, sorted by size and quality, are awaiting export. Published by permission from Stevns Lokalhistoriske Arkiv.

Figure 49 *Rocks and flint nodules present in moraine deposits are exposed as streams erode away the smaller sediment fractions. Beach at Mossby, southern Scania.*

However, circumstances are more favorable on beaches and along streams. Although beach levels during prehistory have shifted considerably over time, we can nevertheless assume that today's observations can have some relevance for investigating prehistoric availability. In some cases prehistoric availability might even have been greater than it is today. For instance, as mentioned earlier, the higher sea level during the Neolithic in northwestern Jutland meant that an archipelago characterized by steep cliffs with layers of accessible primary flint was formed here (Nielsen 1997:262). The Early Neolithic coincided with one of the great transgressions of the Littorina Sea. The rising waters must have eroded many slopes and cliffs composed of chalk and exposed the hard flint layers when the sea level sank again (Becker 1959:92).

Figure 50 *Some of the flint nodules found on the beach at Mossby, Scania.*

A number of systematic field studies with the aim of locating and quantifying flint have been carried out in Scandinavia. Geologist Margit Werner conducted an extensive program of field surveys in the 1960s. Werner's research was designed to establish the source of the flint on the Swedish west coast and to determine how it got there. She carried out an ambitious program of general field survey from the coast and 40 to 50 km inland in Scania, Halland, and Bohuslän. She also conducted field surveys in Denmark and in the area around Oslo in Norway. She surveyed beaches, gravel and clay pits, road cuttings and ploughed fields. Werner counted and weighed all flint and chalk pieces she encountered and recorded the color of the flint, if fossils were present, and the appearance of the cortex.

Werner recorded her observations in tables and on maps. She found that flint is seldom found more than 30 km from the present coastline. The number of finds decreases with increasing height above sea level. Werner did not attempt to record flint type, but noted that most of the flint she encountered was gray. Black and dark gray flints were less common and were evenly distributed. Flint pieces were generally small, less than 15 cm, and nodules weighing more than 500 g were rare. Localities with flint were evenly distributed topographically and flint was encountered at most

1.5 m below the surface. Werner found that gravel-cobble-boulder beaches generally contained more flint than sand beaches. However, she also observed that repeated mapping of the same beach showed that larger rocks were visible on some occasions but covered by sand on others. Werner's conclusion was that the source area of the flint was the shores of the Kattegat Sea after deglaciation. The main agency transporting the flint was ice-rafting (Werner 1974).

Another geologist, Karna Lidmar-Bergström, carried out field survey in southern Sweden during the early 1980s. She was interested in testing the idea that some of the flints in these areas could be of local origin. Along the coast of Halland she recorded the type of deposit, amount of Cretaceous rocks, size of flint nodules, type of flint, and presence of chalk or limestone. She also conducted a systematic search for flint in the area between the Laholm Bay in northwestern Scania and the Kristianstad Plain to the east. Lidmar-Bergström concluded that local flint types exist in southern Halland and these localities are the source of some of the flint in the area (Lidmar-Bergström 1982).

Archaeologist Ulrika Randver recently carried out survey work in the vicinity of three Mesolithic sites in Scania: Tågerup, Rönneholm and Årup (Randver 2004).

Figure 51 Flint-bearing areas along the Swedish west coast, the results of Lidmar-Bergström's field survey. Dots mark places with presumed local provenience of flint. Redrawn from Lidmar-Bergström (1982) and Lidmar-Bergström (1983), with permission.

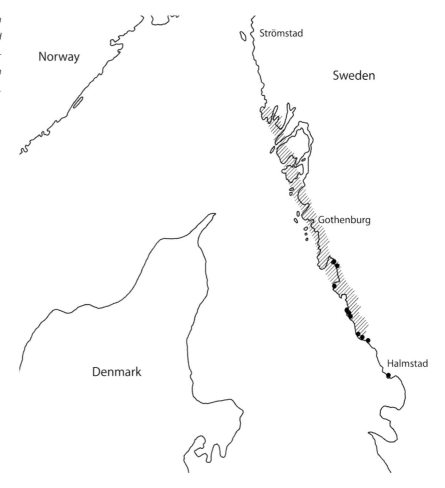

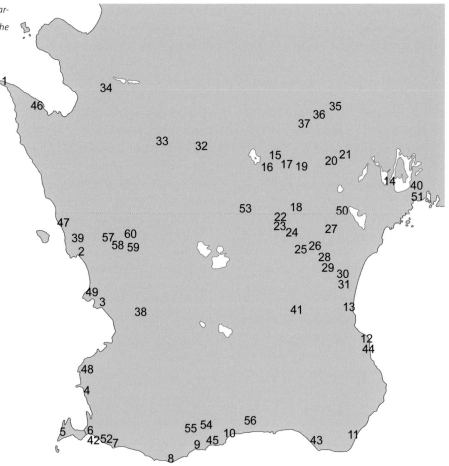

Figure 52 The results of survey work in Scania carried out by Werner (1974), Randver (2004) and the authors, plus information from Hägg (1954).

1 Three beach localities surveyed by Werner. 12 flint nodules were recorded, average weight 53 g.

2 Sand beach at mouth of Saxå River. Surveyed by Randver in 2004. Senonian flint dominated. The largest nodule observed was 45 cm in diameter.

3 Sand beach at the mouth of the Lödde River. Surveyed by Olausson and Högberg in 2004. Largest flint nodule was 40 cm long. Senonian, Danian, and Matte Danian, Östra Torp Variety were found.

4 Sand beach at Eskilstorpsängar. Surveyed by Olausson in 2004. Flint, mostly in the form of smaller pieces, is common here. Scandinavian Senonian, Danian, and Matte Danian, Östra Torp Variety were observed.

5 Beach locality surveyed by Werner. 19 pieces of flint recorded, average weight 39 g.

6 Beach locality surveyed by Werner. 3 pieces of flint recorded, average weight 28 g.

7 Beach locality surveyed by Werner. 6 pieces of flint recorded from the meadow at the beach, average weight 18 g.

8 Beach locality at Östra Torp, surveyed by Högberg and Olausson in 2004. An outcrop of Danian flint, eroded by wave action, was discovered here.

9 Beach locality surveyed by Werner. 13 pieces of flint recorded, average weight 8.5 g.

10 Beach locality at Mossby Strand, surveyed by Högberg and Olausson in 2004. Flint nodules of both Scandinavian Senonian and Matte Danian were common. The largest was 12 cm.

11 Beach locality surveyed by Werner. No flint recorded.

12 Beach locality surveyed by Werner. 3 flints recorded, average weight 28 g.

13 Beach locality at the mouth of the Verke River, surveyed by Högberg and Olausson in 2004. Nodules of Kristianstad flint were common.

14 Beach locality, Lake Ivö, surveyed by Högberg and Olausson in 2004. Flint of very poor quality was observed.

15 Stratigraphic section surveyed by Werner. Moraine. 3 pieces of Kristianstad flint recorded, average weight 63 g, 0 to 4 m below surface.

16 Stratigraphic section surveyed by Werner. 4 pieces of Kristianstad flint recorded, average weight 75 g, 0 to 2 meter below surface.

conditions may differ in some ways from the rest of the formation, although they are similar in other ways (Bush & Sieveking 1986:134; Luedtke 1992:55).

Through the entire Late Cretaceous-Danian time interval the masses surrounding the Danish Basin were flat and low-lying and the climate was arid. As a result, very little terrigenous material reached the shallow epicontinental sea of northwestern Europe (Surlyk & Håkansson 1999). In consequence, the flints here contain low concentrations of trace elements, which places high demands on analytical methods. These must be capable of detecting a large suite of potential elements, even when these occur in low concentrations.

Although geochemical analysis of chalk flint in England and the Netherlands has been carried out in a number of studies (Bush & Sieveking 1986; Craddock, *et al.* 1983; de Bruin, *et al.* 1972; Gardiner 1990; McDonnell, *et al.* 1997; Sieveking, *et al.* 1972), little systematic work designed to characterize the Scandinavian flint sources has been done. Micheelsen performed a wet trace element analysis of specimens of Senonian flint from Stevns Klint, Denmark, in 1966. The results showed that the flint consisted of 98.44 % SiO_2 (Micheelsen 1966:308). Matiskainen *et al.* used atomic absorption spectrometry to analyze 71 samples of flint for 20 chemical elements. Their aim was to identify flint artifacts found on Finnish stone and bronze age sites as being made of either "eastern" (Russian) or "western" (Danish or Swedish) flint. They were able to distinguish between these two on the basis of five elements (Matiskainen, *et al.* 1989). Subsequently, Costopoulos tested new elemental composition data on the same samples using an electron microprobe and energy dispersive spectrometer, and was able to confirm Matiskainen's results (Costopoulos 2003).

ICP-MS analysis

In an attempt to find a reliable method for chemically characterizing Scandinavian flint sources the authors initiated a study of several different Scandinavian flint types using Laser Ablation Inductively Coupled Plasma Mass Spectrometry (LA-ICP-MS). Detection limits for most elements (major, minor, trace and ultra-trace) are much superior for ICP-MS than for other analytical methods. Laser ablation is a technique which is virtually non-destructive to most samples, considering that the ablated areas are often indistinguishable with the naked eye. We submitted 360 flake samples for analysis by LA-ICP-MS to the Research Reactor Center at the University of Missouri-Columbia.

The result was that the markedly high silica concentrations resulted in the dilution of other elements. A further complication was that there appeared to be considerable heterogeneity within the individual sample. Since LA-ICP-MS is equivalent to a microprobe analytical technique, attempts to generate bulk compositional data are challenging. We were forced to conclude that this method was not suitable for these flint types (Speakman 2004; Speakman, *et al.* 2002).

In order to avoid the problems caused by high silica content we decided to try a sampling method which involved ICP-MS of solutions, rather than a microprobe method. We submitted our 360 samples to David S. Wray at the Analytical Unit at the University of Greenwich in Great Britain. Flakes were crushed and treated with hydrofluoric, perchloric and nitric acid in a process which removed the silica. This

Flint	Samples from
Danian	Quarry dump
Danian	Quarry dump
Danian	Chalk cliffs
Danian	Beach outcrop
Senonian	Quarry dump
Senonian	Chalk cliffs
Senonian	Chalk cliffs, layer 1
Senonian	Chalk cliffs, layer 2
Kristianstad	Quarry dump

Figure 53 Provenience of flint samples submitted for ICP-MS analysis.

moved either by solution or by the loosening of the quartz grains so that they fall out. Even in a single flint fragment, variations in texture and microstructure can result in uneven weathering (Luedtke 1992:98–99).

The color of flint can alter into many shades, but there is general agreement that color changes which can occur in dark flints fall into two main categories: white or bleached patina and yellow or brown patina. White patina can appear as a bluish film in its initial stage of development. It can vary in thickness from scarcely measurable to penetrating the whole nodule (Stapert 1976:11). Minor weathering may produce only a bleached and often blotchy surface (Gibbard 1986:143).

Explanations of what causes white patina vary, although most researchers seem to agree that it is primarily an optical phenomenon due to increased porosity which arises as the result of dissolution of silica from between quartz crystals (Gry & Søndergaard 1958; Luedtke 1992; Micheelsen 1966; Schmalz 1960; Stapert 1976). Luedtke reports that scanning electron microscope photographs of white patina show a pitted and porous surface from which light is reflected in all directions (Luedtke 1992:99). Micheelsen used several techniques to establish the possible cause of the white porous crust which had formed on flakes from a Mesolithic deposit found below the present sea level in Denmark. Microscopic examination showed that sea water had dissolved the marginal parts of the flint grains in the white crust. Chemical attack had progressed much more rapidly along grain boundaries than into flint grains. Significantly, X-ray powder diffractograms showed that the leached crust and unleached core were identical in mineral composition (Micheelsen 1966:314).

In contrast to this last observation, Thacker and Ellwood caution against using cortical and weathered surfaces of flint samples for geochemical sourcing. They found that weathering rinds in chert are caused by the leaching of mineral inclusions from weathered surfaces. Paramagnetic and ferromagnetic minerals can easily be lost during the exchange of pore fluids upon exposure during chemical weathering. They conclude that mineral removal, rather than staining or mineral penetration, is the more significant common post depositional process altering chert surfaces (Thacker & Ellwood 2002:476).

Most, but not all, authors claim that white patination occurs mainly in alkaline soils. This is because the solubility of quartz increases with higher pH levels (Hewitt 1915:51; Luedtke 1992:99; Nielsen 1993:16; Stapert 1976:11). As silica is dissolved by an alkaline solvent it has the effect of lowering the pH of the solution until an equilibrium point is reached and silica ceases to dissolve (Schmalz 1960:48). However, Odell cites a study which found no correlation between white patina and soil pH (Odell 2000:270). In fact, Rottländer claims that white patina can form in humic acids under relatively strongly dissolving conditions (Rottländer in: Stapert 1976:12).

Vang Petersen observed that white patina is often present on beach flints, which led him to speculate that sunlight may increase the effects (Vang Petersen 1993:26). Stapert makes the observation that upward facing surfaces of flint in soil exhibit a thicker patina than those facing downwards (Stapert 1976).

The other major category of patina is the dark variety, resulting in colors such as brown, yellow-brown (cf. figure 21), red, or nearly black. Several explanations for

Figure 54 A single broken microblade found in three sections from the Eigil Knut Site, Holm Land, North East Greenland. The microblade is about 4 cm long. Sheila Coulson, who supplied the illustration, relates the following: In the course of refitting material for the analysis of the site these three sections of a microblade were refitted. The refit of such apparently different materials would not normally have been attempted if it had not been for the highly distinct snap. At first it was thought that the opaque materials were patinated. However, the difference in color was explained by the geologist Minik Rosing as being something quite different. The bottom (brown translucent section) was the part that was heavily altered by exposure to the sun. It had been bleached out. The original color of the material was the opaque cream of the top two sections. This is quite an eye-opener for archaeologists. Photograph courtesy of Sheila Coulson and Claus Andreasen. Photograph by John Lee, National Museum of Denmark.

what causes these color changes have been suggested. Many researchers have proposed that it is necessary for the surface of the flint to be rendered porous by weathering before the staining agent can do its work (Hewitt 1915:51; Luedtke 1992:100; Schmalz 1960:49).

Yellow and brown patina is usually explained as the deposition of various oxides and hydroxides of iron from surface water (Becker 1952:68; Gibbard 1986:142; Hewitt 1915:51; Kelly & Hurst 1956:194; Luedtke 1992:100; Rottländer 1975:109; Stapert 1976:13; Vang Petersen 1993:31). Some see manganese or organic matter as possible coloring agents (Gibbard 1986; Hewitt 1915; Luedtke 1992). Rottländer found that in some cases the iron concentration in a colored patina layer on flint was just as high as in a fresh core of the same kind of flint. In this case it appears that iron from the flint became oxidized on the surface, rather than deposited from outside the flint (Luedtke 1992:100; Rottländer 1975; Stapert 1976:13).

Vang Petersen describes a black patina which can occur on Danish flint, causing the flint to resemble obsidian. Black patinated flint can be found near brackish lagoons and in running water. Vang Petersen suggests that black patina is due to sulfur from rotten seaweed and organic matter acting on flint (Vang Petersen 1993:31).

Finally, Vang Petersen identifies "plough patina", rust-colored spots and scratches which can occur on flints from the ploughzone. This discoloration is due to contact with a metal plough or other metal object (Vang Petersen 1993:31).

Flint types, defined by Carl Johan Becker	Definition
1 Kristianstad flint (Kristianstad-flint; Kristianstadsflint)	Matte, gray flint containing white spots.
2 Zealand chalk flint or Zealand Senonian flint (Sjællandsk senonflint; Seeländische Schreibkreide- oder Senonflint)	This type consists of flint which is very homogeneous. Fresh surfaces are shiny. Flakes are usually black or dark gray while larger pieces are lighter in color. The flint may contain irregular dull areas which are lighter. Cortex is thin and clearly demarcated from the flint.
3 Jutish chalk flint or Jutish Senonian flint (Jysk senon-flint; jütländische Schreibkreide- oder Senonflint)	This type is similar in structure and surface texture to Zealand Senonian flint and it can be difficult to differentiate between these types. However, some examples of Jutish Senonian flint contain numerous white spots of varying sizes whereas these are never present on Zealand Senonian flint. Becker refers to this variety as Jutish spotted flint (Jysk prickig flint). Jutish chalk flint is gray, usually dark gray. The cortex is often thin and porous and the cortex on nodules from primary sources retains its chalky surface.
4 Senonian flint, Hov type (Senon-flint af type Hov)	This type is identical to Zealand Senonian flint in respect to color, homogeneity and cortex. It was mined in the Early Neolithic flint mines at Hov, northwestern Jutland.
5 Matte Danian flint (Mat danien-flint; Mattem Danien-Flint)	Light to dark gray flint with a fairly homogeneous but coarse structure.
6 "Clear" Danian flint ("Klar" danien-flint; Klarem Danien-Flint)	Becker characterizes this as a heterogeneous type which is difficult to define. When it lacks cortex it can be difficult to distinguish from Senonian flint but in a fresh state it is light gray and less shiny than Senonian flint. It can contain macroscopic fossils, especially bryozoans. The cortex is always thicker than on Senonian flint. Cortex is very irregular and often consists of silicified limestone.
7 Paleocene ball flint (Paleocen Kugleflint)	Small round nodules of gray or yellowish flint with gray, black or yellow cortex, rolled and eroded in Paleocene riverbeds.

Peter Vang Petersen´s addition	Definition
1 Banded Falster flint (Falsterflint, (båndet))	This variety of Senonian flint can be found in southeastern Denmark. Falster flint is described as banded with a bluish tint. The lighter-colored bands are especially close together near the surface of the nodules.
2 Bryozoan flint (Fynsk bryozoflint)	A type which contains numerous bryozoan fossils. Nodules can vary as to size and shape. Some varities are shiny and transparent, others are dull and more typical of Danian flint varieties. Bryozoan flint is of Danian age.

today in quarry waste at the abutment for the Öresund Bridge. However, another Danian age flint is also present along the coast at Limhamn. This flint was available in prehistory on the beach ridges and it was used for production of for example Neolithic square-sectioned axes. Scandinavian Senonian flint is also present in these beach ridges (Högberg 2002) and many different kinds of flint from various primary sources are present in moraine deposits in the area.

Clearly, the term "Limhamn flint" covers a broad spectrum of many different types of flint and as a classificatory term it is therefore much too broad to be practical. It is not a definition of a flint type and it is only meaningful when used in the sense that Kjellmark did in his description of prehistoric settlements in Blekinge, namely "all types of flint which cannot be classified as Kristianstad flint" (Kjellmark 1939).

Figure 56 Archaeologist Carl Johan Becker's classification into seven types, based on characteristics relevant for archaeologists rather than geologists. Forty years later, archaeologist Peter Vang Petersen (1993) added a further two types.

Figure 57 Samples of Scandinavian Senonian flint collected by the authors and Mikkel Sørensen at Valsømagle, Zealand in Denmark.

Furthermore, we cannot assume that all flint which is called "Limhamn flint" does in fact come from southwestern Scania. The type of flint occurring in the region of Limhamn can also be found on Zealand in Denmark and Rügen in Germany, for example. For these reasons "Limhamn flint" is unsuitable as a classificatory term.

Figure 58 Flint layers of Danian age in the limestone at the Limhamn quarry in southwestern Scania.

Archaeologists from central Sweden also occasionally refer to "chalk flint". This term denotes flint of southern Scandinavian origin and it is mostly used in a sense which excludes the Ordovician and Cambrian flint found on prehistoric sites in central Sweden (Kindgren 1991). It also includes the glacially transported flint occuring along the Swedish west coast and in southern Norway. The problem with the definition is similar to that with the term "Limhamn flint". "Chalk flint" covers a broad spectrum of many different types of flint; e.g., Danian flint from the bedrock of southwestern Scania, Senonian flint from moraine deposits, and Senonian flint from the bedrock in northeastern Scania. It also refers to flint from chalk bedrock, while much of the flint from southwestern Scania; i.e., Danian flint, comes from a limestone bedrock. Therefore, "chalk flint" is also unsuitable as a classificatory term.

Today most Swedish archaeologists content themselves with classification into three types: Senonian, Danian and Kristianstad flint. Swedish archaeologist Bo Knarrström also mentions another type which he calls "flint with rough or transformed structure". This kind of flint has coarser grains and a coarse surface. Knarrström suggests that nodules with this appearance were once ordinary Senonian or Danian flints which have been transformed by long periods in acetous environments (Knarrström 2001:21).

"Hälleflinta" and "leptit" are Swedish terms used for flint-like rocks from central Sweden. These are composed of volcanic ash transformed into a hard rock which resembles flint. The material has been used for tool-making during prehistory (Kindgren 1991), but because it is not flint we have not included it in the present book.

"Moraine flint" is a term used to describe flint found in glacial deposits in southern Sweden, Denmark, and the northern part of the European continent. "Moraine flint" is not a type; rather it is a description of the environment in which the flint can be found. Other terms for "moraine flint" are "Baltic flint" and "erratic flint".

Explanation of the flint registration terminology

The descriptions of the 17 flint types which follow are based on the terminology established and used in the initial sampling work at the flint seminar in May 2001.

Samples Numbers refer to the original flint samples as registered at the flint seminar. We have retained these numbers on the samples in the reference collection.

Name The frequently used or commonly accepted name(s) for the flint in Swedish and Danish are given. We have tried to retain the commonly accepted name in the classification we propose when we have found it adequate. The new terms we propose are mainly descriptive rather than geographical.

Geological age The geological age of formation, when known, is given.

Flint color A description of the color of the fresh flint may be useful in distinguishing flint types, and indeed this is usually one of our main criteria for doing so. However, color can alter due to chemical weathering and patination (see Weathering and patination, above) and it is therefore important to obtain fresh, unpatinated surfaces for color comparisons. It has unfortunately not been possible to do this for the types from secondary sources we have included. For these types the color we describe is altered by patination and cannot be assumed to be the original color. Also it is important to bear in mind that since many flint types are transparent, the thickness of the flake can affect our impression of color – thinner flakes can look lighter than thicker pieces, which absorb more light. We rejected use of the Munsell Color Chart for color registration as being too cumbersome.

Flint structure This variable corresponds to what Crabtree calls texture (Crabtree 1967). Crabtree writes that textures range from very glassy or vitreous to more granular. The definition of grain size is based on how we perceive a noncortical surface, normally the ventral surface on a flake. Luedtke has shown that what is actually described by looking at the structure this way is the fractured surface, not the grain size. The largest quartz grains are normally only c. 0.05 mm in diameter and cannot be distinguished by the naked eye (Luedtke 1992:65). Nevertheless, we have chosen to describe structure in terms of grain size since we feel there is some consensus among archaeologists about what this means. We have registered our impression of the grain size on a scale from fine to coarse.

Flaked surface A description of the tactile impression of the freshly flaked surface. The choices are:
- smooth or glassy,
- scalar – feels like fish scales,
- gritty, or
- plastic – the grains have melted together and the material feels like it is molded.

Reflectivity registers an impression of how much light is reflected from a fresh surface. We have registered our impressions as shiny or matte.

Homogeneity refers to the uniformity of the flint matrix. A homogeneous material is one in which the composition and the physical state are uniform throughout (Crabtree 1967). If fossils are visible to the naked eye we have noted this here.

Bryozoan fossils are present in some flints. The term "bryozoan" as used by archaeologists does not necessarily correspond to the geological terminology. In the archaeological parlance it denotes small rods of lighter-colored material and it is in this looser sense we use it here.

Translucency refers to the light transmission qualities of the flint, determined by holding a thin flake against a light source.

The **cortex** is the exterior surface layer of the nodule. Luedtke advocates reserving the term "cortex" for the layer that forms on the outer surface of a nodule or bed during diagenesis (Luedtke 1992:67). Authors differ in their explanations of the chemical composition of the cortex. Gry & Søndergaard (1958) suggest it consists of chalcedony or opal. Luedtke writes that the cortex is chemically intermediate between the chert and its matrix and therefore it is distinct from either the chert or its matrix (Luedtke 1992:67). A nodule which is freshly removed from its matrix of limestone or chalk may retain some of this matrix on its surface.

On the unweathered nodule the appearance of the cortex may be an important clue about flint type. Mechanical weathering can, however, radically alter cortex appearance and thickness and it can in practice be difficult to distinguish between chalk and limestone on weathered pieces. Archaeologists generally assume that the presence of a chalky cortex means that the flint has been freshly extracted from the chalk. However Briggs (1986:187) claims to have observed chalk adhering to drift flints which have traveled great distances.

In our classifications we have distinguished among three possible **conditions** for cortex:
- chalky – leaves a chalk residue upon the fingers when a fresh surface is rubbed,
- limestone – hard and stony, and
- weathered – not possible to distinguish the original cortex of the sample due to weathering.

We have also described the surface **structure** of the unweathered cortex, distinguishing among:
- soft – can be scratched with the fingernail, or hard – impervious to scratching,
- smooth or rough, referring to the microtopography, and
- regular or irregular, whether the cortex is even or uneven in thickness; macrotopography.

The **thickness** of the cortex is measured when possible and the **color** of the unweathered cortex is recorded. In some cases we have been unable to obtain cortical nodules from a primary source. In such cases we describe the color of the weathered cortex.

In our attempts to distinguish flint types we noted that an important characteristic was the appearance of the **transition zone** between the flint and the cortex. We have therefore tried to describe this for each type in as much detail as possible.

Nodule form and dimensions Nodule form is described using the terms rounded, tabular, loaf-shaped, hambone, or irregular. Estimates of the largest dimension of smallest and largest known nodules are given.

If there are particular **distinguishing characteristics** we note them.

An important characteristic for the prehistoric knapper to consider was the tractability of the raw material. We have therefore attempted to record the relative **knappability** of each flint sample, plotting this on a scale from brittle to tough. Knappability encompasses Crabtree's variables "resistance to shock", "elasticity" and "flexibility" (Crabtree 1967). Crabtree notes that the finer the flint's texture, the greater the knapper's control in making flakes, blades and tools. An evaluation of knappability therefore encompasses many of the characteristics we have also evaluated separately

Figure 59 A biface made of Common Kristianstad Flint by Bruce Bradley in 1999. Bradley is a highly skilled flintknapper with many years' experience.

Figure 60 Some researchers have stated that Kristianstad flint is of poor quality and therefore unsuitable for manufacturing Neolithic square-sectioned axes. Our research has proved this to be incorrect. The photograph shows three Neolithic axes made of Common Kristianstad Flint from the collection in the Regional Museum, Kristianstad. The axe to the left is c. 10 cm long. Photo by Ylva Sundgren, Regional Museum, Kristianstad.

such as **flint structure** and **flaked surface**. Högberg knapped a few flakes from each sample so that we could minimize intersubjectivity in this variable. We also recorded any information we had regarding the material's suitability for knapping as well as our judgement about any effects the cortex may have on knappability.

Location of the reference sample The collection point for each sample is marked on a map.

Geographical distribution pattern This relates to the known geological occurrence of the flint. This information has been gleaned from published sources, from our own field investigations, and from the information gained at the seminar. As far as possible we have attempted to describe the **primary** and **secondary occurrence** of the flint type, when known. The **present accessibility** of the flint type is recorded from the information given by our informants and from survey work (see Availability, above), while our estimates of the **prehistoric accessibility** are of course hypotheses.

Figure 61 *A bifacially knapped, polished and pressure-flaked Bronze Age spearhead made from Common Kristianstad Flint, c. 8 cm long. Photo by Christer Åhlin, Museum of National Antiquities, Sweden.*

Information on the **use of the flint** has been gained through informants and from published work. This is not an exhaustive list. Specific references to the type of flint are given under **published references**. A bibliography listing the more general references to flint, as well as all cited work, is provided at the conclusion of the book. We present flint appearance as accurately as possible; photographs vary in scale.

Kristianstad Flint

Kristianstad flint has traditionally been considered easy to recognize as a type and fairly homogeneous. However, in our work we have found that there is some variation in the flint, especially regarding the color of the matrix and the appearance of the lighter spots. We therefore distinguish two varieties of Kristianstad flint – Common Kristianstad Flint and Black Kristianstad Flint. Common Kristianstad Flint shows a wide range of variation. All varieties of Common Kristianstad Flint have lighter colored spots of various sizes in a matrix which varies from dark to light gray. Black Kristianstad Flint is characterized by a deep black color and by an almost total absence of spots.

Among some modern knappers and archaeologists, Common Kristianstad Flint is characterized as tough and somewhat intractable (Högberg 1997:37). However at least two modern flintknappers, Bruce Bradley and Bo Madsen (Madsen 1984), disagree with this assessment; in fact Bradley was able to apply bifacial technique on Common Kristianstad Flint with good results, figure 59. Archaeologists have also assumed that Kristianstad flint occurs only in small nodules but our survey work has demonstrated that it can occur in very large nodules of good quality (Högberg 2005).

Black Kristianstad Flint, not previously described by archaeologists, differs quite markedly from all previously published descriptions of Kristianstad flint. It is of high quality and easily worked. Dan Kärrefors, an experienced modern knapper, reports that it is suitable for both blade production and for making square-sectioned axes (Kärrefors 2001).

Figure 62 *Two preforms for Neolithic square-sectioned axes made of Kristianstad flint found in the parish of Norra Åsum in Scania. The one above is made of Black Kristianstad Flint. It is c. 20 cm long. When this type of flint is polished or patinated it is very difficult to distinguish from Scandinavian Senonian Flint. Photo by Christer Åhlin, Museum of National Antiquities, Sweden.*

Common Kristianstad Flint

Samples 3, 7, and 8

Name

This is the "classic" variety of Kristianstad flint. Characteristic for the flint is the numerous lighter colored spots of various sizes in a black or gray matrix.

Geological age

Campanian.

Use of the flint

Mesolithic flake axes and other small tools such as small blades, scrapers, and drills. Core axes (Cederschiöld 1949), square-section axes (Knarrström 1997), Late Neolithic daggers (Apel 2001), and large blade knives from the Late Bronze Age (Högberg 2005) are known. Many of the artifacts of Common Kristianstad Flint occur in unpublished private collections (Strömberg 1952).

Published references

Cederschiöld 1949, 1950.
Madsen 1984.
Wyszomirska 1988.

Geographical distribution pattern

NE Scania, Sweden.

Primary occurrence

Limestone layers at Hanaskog, Sweden. Also occurs in other areas with limestone layers in the region north of Kristianstad, Sweden.

Secondary occurrence

According to Carserud (1994) this flint can occur in Scania's moraine deposits from northeastern Scania and Blekinge to southwestern Scania.

Present accessibility

Easily accessible at quarry sites and in ploughed fields near these.

Prehistoric accessibility

This flint is quite common in moraines. Högberg's field survey in ploughed fields near the Hanaskog quarry revealed large quantities of debitage of this flint from the manufacture of Late Bronze Age large blade knives. This leads us to conclude that, at least in Late Bronze Age, people had access to the outcrop (Högberg 2005). The extent of prehistoric accessibility is not directly known, however.

Location of reference samples

Sample 3, limestone quarry at Hanaskog, Sweden.
Sample 7, limestone quarry at Hanaskog, Sweden.
Sample 8, Östra Sönnarslöv, Sweden.

Flint color

Black or dark gray matrix speckled with numerous gray, white or yellowish-white spots of different sizes consisting of unsilicified calcium.

Flint structure

Fine  Coarse

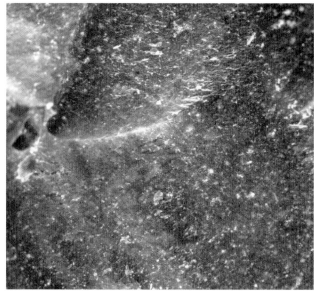

Flaked surface

Scalar and gritty.

Reflectivity

Matte.

Homogeneity

The matrix is very homogeneous and fossils are rare.

Translucency

Opaque.

Nodule form and dimensions

A variety of nodule forms occur: hambone, rounded, and irregular. From handball-sized to very large nodules. We have discovered nodules up to more than one meter in size at the modern quarry at Hanaskog, Sweden.

Other distinguishing characteristics

None.

Knappability

Brittle  Tough

The material is easily worked but fragile and it requires good technique. Well-prepared platforms are necessary for maintaining control. The thick and irregular cortex may hinder knapping. The diving cortex intruding into the flint also makes knapping more difficult.

Cortex condition

Limestone.

Cortex structure

Hard, smooth or rough, irregular.

Cortex thickness

5 to 30 mm.

Cortex color

Gray or yellowish-white.

Transition

The transition between flint and cortex is distinct. In some areas the gray spots are more frequent at the transition. Rods and pockets of cortex "dive" into the body of the flint.

Black Kristianstad Flint

Name

This is a variety of Kristianstad flint which to our knowledge has not previously been described by archaeologists. As the name suggests, Black Kristianstad Flint is characterized by a deep, matte black color with very few of the gray and yellow spots which generally have been regarded as being so characteristic of Kristianstad flint. Although Swedish geologist Anders Henning described this flint in an article in 1895 (Henning 1895), archaeologists have not previously been aware of its existence.

Geological age

Campanian.

Use of the flint

Use is unknown since this type has not previously been identified by archaeologists. We have found one Neolithic square-sectioned axe preform made of this flint, see figure 62.

Published references

Henning 1895.

Geographical distribution pattern
  NE Scania, Sweden.

Primary occurrence
  In limestone layers at Hanaskog, Sweden.

Secondary occurrence
  Unknown. This flint type has not been identified in secondary occurrences.

Present accessibility
  Accessible in the quarry.

Prehistoric accessibility
  Unknown.

Location of reference samples
  Sample 1, limestone quarry at Hanaskog, Sweden.

Black Kristianstad Flint

Flint color

Black with rare gray spots of unsilicified calcium 5 to 10 mm in diameter.

Flint structure

Fine  Coarse

Flaked surface

Glassy and plastic.

Reflectivity

Shiny.

Homogeneity

The flint is very homogeneous and no fossils are visible.

Translucency

Opaque.

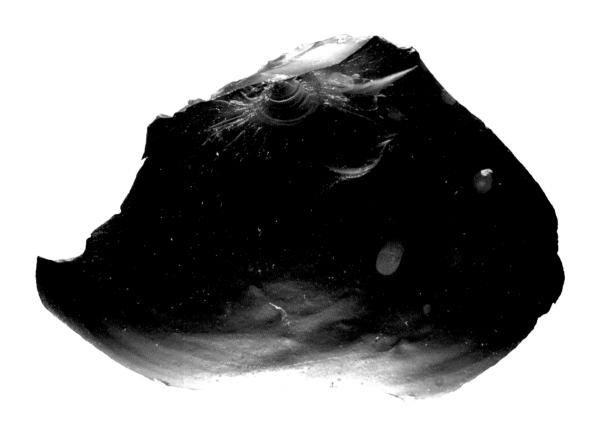

Nodule form and dimensions
Rounded or irregular nodules. Handball-sized to very large.

Other distinguishing characteristics
None.

Knappability

Brittle  Tough

The material is very easily worked. It is slightly tough, homogeneous, and excellent for knapping. In those cases when the cortex and the flint blend together, both the darker and the lighter areas react the same way to knapping and a knapped edge in the gray area is as sharp as an edge in the black area.

Cortex condition
Limestone.

Cortex structure
Hard, smooth, irregular.

Cortex thickness
5 to 30 mm.

Cortex color
Yellowish gray.

Transition
Two varieties have been observed:
- very sharp boundary between flint and cortex, or
- an area of 5 to 10 mm where the flint and the cortex blend together. In this area the structure is the same but the color grades from black to lighter gray.

Scandinavian Senonian Flint

Name

Scandinavian Senonian Flint is the most common of the southern Scandinavian flint types. The type includes Becker's (1988) type 2 Zealand Senonian flint, type 4 Senonian flint, Hov type, and type 3 Jutish Senonian flint. Our observations have led us to the conclusion that these varieties are not sufficiently different to warrant putting them into separate categories. We do not include the speckled variety Becker calls Jutish spotted flint here.

It should be noted that many authors in English-speaking publications (e.g. Luedtke 1992; Micheelsen 1966; Sieveking, *et al.* 1972) use the term "Stevns flint" to refer to this kind of flint. However this term is misleading, because there are outcrops of both Scandinavian Senonian Flint and Gray Band Danian Flint in the chalk and limestone layers at Stevns Klint, Denmark, see figures 26 and 27. In at least one publication this flint is referred to as "Nordic flint" (http://flintsource.net).

Sw. *Senonflinta, Sallerupsflinta, Ängdalaflinta.*

Dk. *Sjællandsk senonflint, Senon-flint af type Hov, Jysk senonflint, Bjerre flint, Valsømagle flint.*

Geological age

Maastrichtian.

Use of the flint

Widely used in prehistory for all types of tools.

Published references

Althin 1951.

Apel 2001.

Becker 1980a, 1980b, 1988, 1990, 1993.

Berthelsen 1993.

Glob 1951.

Gry & Søndergaard 1958.

Holst 1906.

Jansson 1999.

Madsen 1993.

Nielsen & Rudebeck 1991.

Rudebeck 1981, 1987, 1994, 1998.

Rudebeck, *et al.* 1980.

Steinberg & Pletka 1997.

Thomsen 2000.

Vang Petersen 1993.

Vemming Hansen & Madsen 1983.

Wienberg Rasmussen 1970.

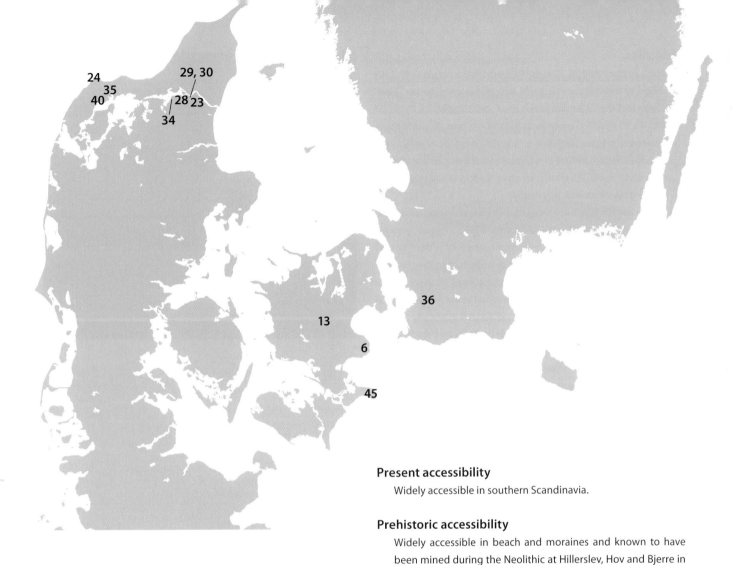

Present accessibility
Widely accessible in southern Scandinavia.

Prehistoric accessibility
Widely accessible in beach and moraines and known to have been mined during the Neolithic at Hillerslev, Hov and Bjerre in Denmark and Södra Sallerup in Sweden.

Location of reference samples
Sample 6, beach at Stevns Klint, eastern Zealand, Denmark.
Sample 13, quarry at Valsømagle, central Zealand, Denmark.
Sample 23, quarry at Rørdal, NE Jutland, Denmark.
Sample 24, quarry at Bjerre, NW Jutland, Denmark.
Sample 28, quarry in Ålborg area, NE Jutland, Denmark.
Sample 29, quarry at Ellidshøj/Mjels, NE Jutland, Denmark.
Sample 30, quarry at Ellidshøj, NE Jutland, Denmark.
Sample 34, beach at Nibe, NE Jutland, Denmark.
Sample 35, flint mine at Hov, NW Jutland, Denmark.
Sample 36, quarry at Södra Sallerup, SW Sweden.
Sample 40, quarry at Kjelstrup, NW Jutland, Denmark.
Sample 45, beach at Møns Klint, Møn, Denmark.

Geographical distribution pattern
Southwestern Sweden and northern Jutland, Møn and eastern Zealand in Denmark.

Primary occurrence
Geological deposits in chalk cliffs at Stevns Klint, Møns Klint, and in the Thisted structure in northern Jutland, Denmark.

Secondary occurrence
Chalk slabs at Södra Sallerup and in moraines in SW Sweden; moraines and beach ridges in northern Jutland, Zealand and on Møn, Denmark.

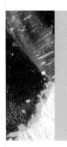

Speckled Senonian Flint

Name

Becker sees this as a variety of his type 3 Jutish Senonian flint. Petersen and Becker refer to it as Jutish spotted Senonian flint (Becker 1988; Vang Petersen 1993). Characteristic are the numerous light gray spots in a darker matrix, giving the flint the appearance of a starry sky. Occasionally Scandinavian Senonian Flint can have scattered lighter spots. The difference is that Speckled Senonian Flint has distinct gray spots in a black matrix whereas if small spots are present in Scandinavian Senonian Flint they usually occur in a gray matrix.

Dk. *Gølflint; jysk småprikket senonflint.*

Geological age

Maastrichtian.

Use of the flint

Widely used in prehistory for all types of tools, including axes, daggers and sickles.

Published references

Becker 1980b, 1988, 1993.
Kragh 1964.
Thomsen 2000.
Vang Petersen 1993.

Geographical distribution pattern

Northern Jutland, Denmark.

Primary occurrence

Chalk deposits in northern Jutland, Denmark.

Secondary occurrence

Moraines in central and northern Jutland, Denmark.

Present accessibility

Widely accessible in Thy and northern Jutland, Denmark.

Prehistoric accessibility

Widely accessible in Thy and northern Jutland. Becker (1993) suggests that Gøl flint was being mined prehistorically, although such mines have not yet been located.

Location of reference samples

Sample 22, quarry at Hillerslev, NW Jutland, Denmark.
Sample 32, quarry at Gøl, NE Jutland, Denmark.
Sample 46, quarry at Ellidshøj, NE Jutland, Denmark.

Flint color
Dark gray with numerous lighter spots.

Flint structure

Fine  Coarse

Flaked surface
Smooth and glassy.

Reflectivity
Shiny.

Homogeneity
Homogeneous.

Translucency
Highly translucent.

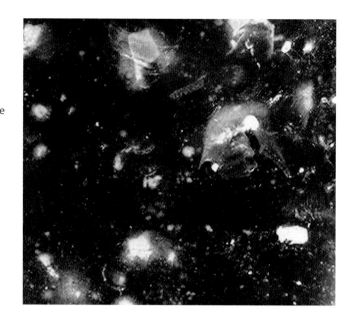

Nodule form and dimensions

Irregular or tabular; nodules vary from fist-sized to 50 cm.

Other distinguishing characteristics

The lighter spots in the dark flint are usually very small, c. 1 mm. They can occur separately, be concentrated into "galaxies", or arranged lineally. There are occasional small pockets of chalk in the flint.

Knappability

Brittle 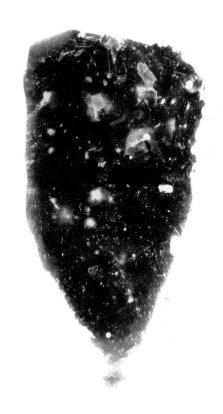 Tough

The flint is of very good quality, suitable for all types of tools. A thicker cortex can adversely affect knapping.

Cortex condition

Chalky.

Cortex structure

Soft, smooth, regular.

Cortex thickness

5 to 20 mm.

Cortex color

White.

Transition

The transition between flint and cortex is ragged – a strip of lighter flint "drips" into the darker flint.

Falster Flint

Sample 10

Name

The most striking characteristic of this flint is its blue striped appearance. Falster flint is abundant in clearance cairns on the island of Falster and the former island of Hasselø, Denmark. Farmers here complain that the nodules are so large that the plough does not move them and the sharp edges of flaked flint slice holes in tractor tires, see figures 35 & 45.

Sw. *Falsterflinta.*

Dk. *Stribet falsterflint, blå falsterflint.*

Geological age

Maastrichtian.

Use of the flint

This flint has been used for all types of prehistoric artifacts.

Published references

Madsen 1993.

Thomsen 2000.

Vang Petersen 1993.

Geographical distribution pattern

Falster, Lolland, and southern Zealand in Denmark.

Primary occurrence

In chalk three to four meters under the surface in southern Zealand and on Falster, Denmark.

Secondary occurrence

Moraine near the chalk on Falster, Lolland and Zealand, Denmark.

Present accessibility

Two modern open quarries at Hasselø on Falster are now filled with water. Therefore, the flint is not available in outcrops but it occurs abundantly in the moraine and is common on the surface and in clearance cairns.

Prehistoric accessibility

Probably available in moraines and on beaches.

Location of reference samples

Sample 10, Hasselø on the island of Falster, Denmark.

Flint color

Blue, black, or gray with stripes of lighter flint.

Flint structure

Fine  Coarse

Flaked surface

Glassy.

Reflectivity

Shiny.

Homogeneity

Generally very homogeneous with occasional patches of coarser flint. Occasional crystallized fossils are visible.

Translucency

Highly translucent.

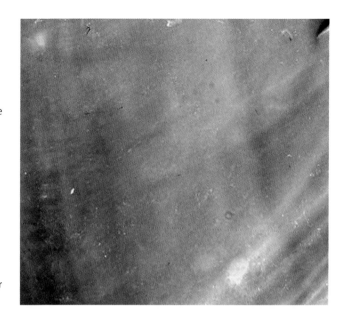

Nodule form and dimensions

Nodules are round or irregular. The largest known nodules are up to 1 m in size.

Other distinguishing characteristics

The most distinguishing characteristic is the flint's striped appearance. However, not all areas of the flint are striped and when stripes are absent it is difficult to distinguish the dark varieties of this type from Scandinavian Senonian Flint.

Knappability

Brittle  Tough

The flint is very easily worked and force travels easily. The patches of lighter material are somewhat tougher but since the nodules are large and the flint is otherwise of good quality this is not usually a problem for the knapper. The cortex does not affect knapping.

Cortex condition

Chalky or weathered.

Cortex structure

Hard, smooth, regular.

Cortex thickness

1 to 3 mm.

Cortex color

White.

Transition

The boundary between the flint and the cortex is very distinct.

Rügen Flint

Name

The flint is very similar in appearance to Scandinavian Senonian Flint. However, Rügen Flint has a "diving cortex"; that is, the chalk cortex intrudes into the flint from the surface, building concavities and tunnels in the flint.

Geological age

Maastrichtian.

Use of the flint

In the archaeological literature there is some discussion about whether or not flint from Rügen was used in prehistory. Our own observations of collections at Ernst Moritz Arndt University in Greifswald, Germany revealed several axes and daggers which were made from what appears to be Rügen flint.

Published references

Herrig 1995.
Rassmann 2000.

25

Geographical distribution pattern
Rügen, Germany.

Primary occurrence
Chalk cliffs on Rügen's northeastern coast.

Secondary occurrence
Beaches below the chalk cliffs and in the moraine above them.

Present accessibility
Easily accessible at the chalk cliffs.

Prehistoric accessibility
Probably easily accessible at chalk cliffs and in the moraine.

Location of reference samples
Sample 25, chalk cliffs at Jasmund, northeastern Rügen, Germany.

Flint color

Gray-black, dark gray, gray with a faint brown tinge; some varieties contain light gray spots of variable size.

Flint structure

Fine  Coarse

Flaked surface

In most cases smooth but samples 39 and 47 are somewhat gritty and scalar.

Reflectivity

Shiny.

Homogeneity

Homogeneous except for occasional pockets of chalk.

Translucency

Opaque.

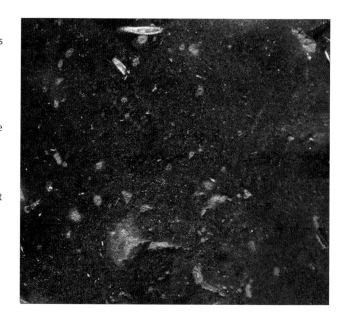

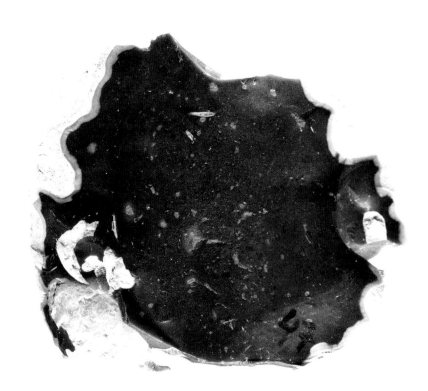

Nodule form and dimensions

Irregular, nodules vary from fist-sized to 1 m. Observed in continuous beds in modern quarries, see figure 58.

Other distinguishing characteristics

Random pockets of chalk in the flint are typical.

Knappability

Brittle   Tough

The irregular configuration of the nodule and cortex makes it difficult to predict the mass of flint within each nodule, making knapping difficult. A thick cortex and pockets of chalk are also detrimental. The flint itself is of good quality. The band of lighter-colored flint just below the cortex reacts to knapping in the same way as the darker flint.

Cortex condition

Limestone.

Cortex structure

All variations in cortex structure have been noted on our samples.

Cortex thickness

Variable, from 1 mm to 10 cm.

Cortex color

White or grayish-white.

Transition

The most characteristic aspect of the flint is the gray or white band between the flint and the cortex. Vang Petersen (1993) calls this silicified transition (Dk. *forkislet overgang*). It varies in width from 1.5 to 3 mm and on some pieces it disappears occasionally. The transitions between the gray band, the cortex, and the body of the flint are distinct.

Gray Band Matte Danian Flint

Name

This flint has not previously been classified as a separate type. Becker (1988) considered it to belong to type 5 Matte Danian flint. Here we have chosen to define this variety as a separate type, distinguished from other matte Danian types by the distinctive gray band between the flint and the cortex.

Geological age

Danian.

Use of the flint

Square-sectioned axes.

Published references

Becker 1988.
Thomsen 2000.
Vang Petersen 1993.

Geographical distribution pattern
Northern Jutland, Denmark.

Primary occurrence
Northwestern Denmark.

Secondary occurrence
Moraines in western Denmark and in southwestern Scania, Sweden; also embedded in limestone blocks redeposited on or near the surface in southwestern Scania.

Present accessibility
Modern quarries in NW Jutland, Denmark.

Prehistoric accessibility
Not known.

Location of reference samples
Sample 20, Hjerm, NW Jutland, Denmark.
Sample 21, quarry at Mønsted, NW Jutland, Denmark.
Sample 49, quarry at Sevel, near Hjerm, NW Jutland, Denmark.

Gray Band Matte Danian Flint

Flint color
Gray.

Flint structure
Fine  Coarse

Flaked surface
Gritty.

Reflectivity
Matte.

Homogeneity
Homogeneous matrix. Occasional fossil inclusions.

Translucency
Opaque.

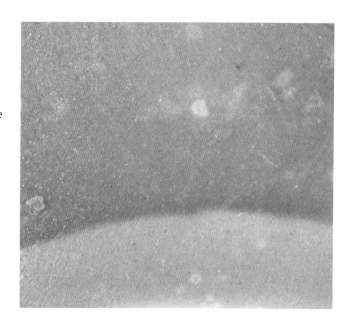

Nodule form and dimensions

Tabular, nodules vary from fist-sized to 50 cm. Observed in continuous beds in modern quarries.

Other distinguishing characteristics

None.

Knappability

Brittle   Tough

The flint can be characterized as hard and tough but of very good quality. It is suitable for all types of tools, especially axes. The cortex poses no problems for knapping.

Cortex condition

Limestone.

Cortex structure

Hard, rough or smooth, regular or irregular.

Cortex thickness

1 mm.

Cortex color

White or yellowish-white.

Transition

The most characteristic aspect of the flint is the gray band between the flint and the cortex. This varies in width but can be up to c. 7 mm. The transitions between the gray band and the cortex on the one hand, and the gray band and the body of the flint on the other, are distinct.

Matte Danian Flint, Östra Torp Variety

Name

This variety of flint has not previously been classified as a separate type. In structure it lies between Gray Band Matte Danian and Gray Band Danian Flint, but it lacks the gray band characteristic of these. The color of the matrix resembles that of Gray Band Danian Flint. Outcrops of this type of flint are visible on the beach at Östra Torp in southern Sweden. This is to our knowledge the only place in southern Sweden where flint in bedrock is available at the surface, see figure 44.

Geological age

Danian.

Use of the flint

Square-sectioned axes and bifacial tools. Both at Östra Torp and at Klagshamn this flint was used in modern times for making flint "bricks".

Published references

Hansen 1929.
Högberg 1999, 2001, 2004.
Kjellmark 1905.
Salomonsson 1971.

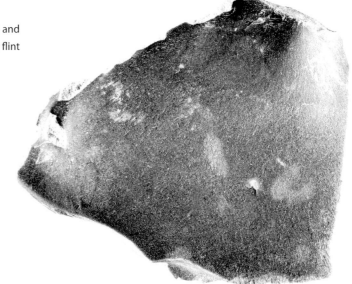

Geographical distribution pattern
SW Sweden.

Primary occurrence
In limestone deposits just below the ploughzone at Sibbarp, SW Sweden; in limestone deposits in the sea and at the beach at Östra Torp; and at the limestone quarry at Klagshamn, Sweden.

Secondary occurrence
In moraines and beach ridges in SW Sweden.

Present accessibility
Easily accessible in the moraine and along the beaches.

Prehistoric accessibility
Beaches, beach ridges and moraine.

Location of reference samples
Sample 33, beach ridge at Sibbarp, SW Sweden.

Sample 37, limestone quarry at Klagshamn, SW Sweden.

Sample 52, limestone quarry at Östra Torp, southern Sweden.

Flint color

Gray to dark gray. Some examples have a marbled appearance.

Flint structure

Fine  Coarse

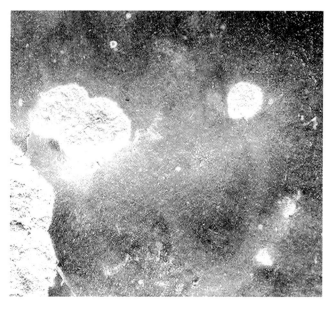

Flaked surface

Gritty and scalar.

Reflectivity

Matte.

Homogeneity

Homogeneous matrix with patches of coarser flint. No fossil inclusions.

Translucency

Opaque.

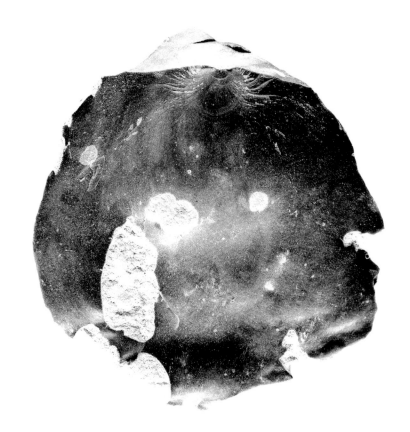

Nodule form and dimensions

Irregular or hambone. Nodules vary in size from beach pebbles and upwards to 50 cm and they may weigh up to 9 kg. Wave action has exposed beds of this flint on the beach at Östra Torp, southern Sweden.

Other distinguishing characteristics

The flint has numerous concavities lined with cortex intruding into the flint.

Knappability

Brittle  Tough

The flint can be characterized as hard and tough, although we have observed variation between nodules with some being more brittle than others. The thick and irregular cortex, in combination with the numerous concavities of cortex intruding into the flint, make production of large objects difficult.

Cortex condition

Limestone.

Cortex structure

Hard, rough, irregular.

Cortex thickness

5 to 40 mm.

Cortex color

White or light gray.

Transition

The transition between flint and cortex is distinct. No gray band is present.

Bryozoan Flint, Funen Variety

Sample 16

Name

The most characteristic aspect of the flint is the numerous bryozoan fossils. Because of the bryozoan fossils it contains, archaeologists and geologists have identified this type as one of the few south Scandinavian flints which is distinctive as to appearance and geological source (Thomsen 2000:35). Our work has shown that not all flint from the geological layers in which this flint occurs has this same, distinctive appearance, however. When visiting the type site at the modern quarry at Klintholm on eastern Funen we found flint which looked like Scandinavian Senonian Flint in the same layers as flint belonging to the type we have called Bryozoan Flint, Funen Variety, see figure 63 on page 148. Dk. *Fynsk bryozoflint*.

Geological age

Danian.

Use of the flint

Square-sectioned axes, blades, and other tools.

Published references

Johansen 1987.
Thomsen 2000.
Vang Petersen 1993.

Geographical distribution pattern

Small nodules are widely distributed in moraines in eastern Denmark and Scania. Large nodules are found primarily on Funen, Denmark.

Primary occurrence

Klintholm, Denmark.

Secondary occurrence

Klintholm, Denmark, beach ridges and moraines.

Present accessibility

Large nodules are found at Klintholm, Denmark, small nodules in moraines.

Prehistoric accessibility

On beach ridges and in moraine in eastern Denmark and Scania.

Location of reference samples

Sample 16, modern quarry at Klintholm, eastern Funen, Denmark.

Flint color

Grayish-brown, speckled.

Flint structure

Fine  Coarse

Flaked surface

From scalar and gritty to smooth and glassy.

Reflectivity

Matte.

Homogeneity

Heterogeneous structure with numerous bryozoan fossils of varying sizes.

Translucency

Highly translucent.

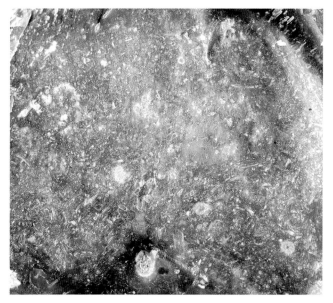

Nodule form and dimensions

Nodules are tabular, rounded, or irregular. The nodules vary from fist-sized up to 50 cm.

Other distinguishing characteristics

None.

Knappability

Brittle  Tough

Despite the numerous bryozoan fossils the flint is very easily knapped. It is suitable for bifacial flaking. The cortex does not affect knapping.

Cortex condition

Chalky or weathered, with visible bryozoan fossils.

Cortex structure

The fresh cortex is soft, somewhat rough, and irregular.

Cortex thickness

1 to 20 mm.

Cortex color

White.

Transition

Sharp transition between flint and cortex. Just under the cortex, in a zone about 5 to 10 mm wide, the flint is darker and more homogeneous and contains few visible bryozoans.

Brown Bryozoan Flint

Name

Archaeologists refer to this flint as "Faxe flint", after a primary source at Fakse, southern Zealand. Another variety of the same type can be found at Vokslev, NE Jutland, Denmark.

Sw. *Faxeflinta.*

Dk. *Faxe flint, Vokslev flint.*

Geological age

Danian.

Use of the flint

Axes, bifacial tools, blades.

Published references

Johansen 1987.

Thomsen 2000.

Vang Petersen 1993.

Weisgerber 1980.

"Fakse Kalkbrud"

http://www.aabne-samlinger.dk/oestsjaellands/kalkbrud.htm

Geographical distribution pattern

Zealand and Jutland, Denmark.

Primary occurrence

Limestone quarry at Fakse; quarry at Vokslev, Denmark.

Secondary occurrence

Moraine deposits on Zealand and northern Jutland, Denmark.

Present accessibility

Modern quarries in the area around Fakse and Vokslev, Denmark.

Prehistoric accessibility

Probably prehistorically available on beaches and in the moraine, although as far as we know this has not been investigated.

Location of reference samples

Sample 4, limestone quarry at Fakse, southern Zealand, Denmark.
Sample 26, quarry at Vokslev, NE Jutland, Denmark.

Flint color

Honey-brown or gray.

Flint structure

Fine  Coarse

Flaked surface

Glassy and slightly gritty.

Reflectivity

Shiny.

Homogeneity

The flint is homogeneous with numerous bryozoans visible to the naked eye.

Translucency

Slightly translucent.

Nodule form and dimensions

Nodules are tabular. The largest nodules are 50 cm. Observed as beds in the quarry at Fakse, see figure 34.

Other distinguishing characteristics

Occasional opalized zones.

Knappability

Brittle   Tough

The flint is easily worked. The thick, regular, chalky cortex cushions the blow but does not negatively affect knapping.

Cortex condition

Chalky.

Cortex structure

Soft, rough, regular.

Cortex thickness

5 to 10 mm.

Cortex color

White.

Transition

The boundary between the flint and the cortex is distinct. In a 10 mm zone under the cortex the flint is yellow and the visible bryozoans are less frequent.

Coarse Bryozoan Flint

Name

Coarse Bryozoan Flint contains clearly visible bryozoan fossils and has a heterogeneous structure.

Geological age

Danian.

Use of the flint

Prehistoric use of this flint has not been documented.

Published references

Johansen 1987.
Thomsen 2000.
Vang Petersen 1993.
Weisgerber 1980.

Geographical distribution pattern
Not documented.

Primary occurrence
In limestone cliffs at Sangstrup Klint, eastern Jutland, Denmark and a limestone quarry at Helligkilde, western Jutland, Denmark.

Secondary occurrence
Not known.

Present accessibility
See above.

Prehistoric accessibility
Flint which eroded from the limestone cliffs at Sangstrup Klint, Denmark would have been available to prehistoric people.

Location of reference samples
Sample 17, limestone cliff at Sangstrup Klint, eastern Jutland, Denmark.
Sample 51, quarry at Helligkilde, western Jutland, Denmark.

Flint color

Light brown or gray.

Flint structure

Fine  Coarse

Flaked surface

Scalar and gritty with irregular structural planes.

Reflectivity

Shiny.

Homogeneity

Heterogeneous structure with pockets of limestone, crystals and fissures. Bryozoan fossils are numerous.

Translucency

High translucency, except where the bryozoans are numerous.

Nodule form and dimensions

Nodules are very irregular. The nodules vary from fist-sized to 20 cm. Observed in beds in quarries and cliffs.

Other distinguishing characteristics

This flint has an extremely heterogeneous structure and contains faults and irregularities. Some fracture patterns are conchoidal while others follow natural bedding planes.

Knappability

Brittle  Tough

The variable fracture patterns make it impossible to predict knapping results. Other difficulties are the variable cortex and the fact that the mass of flint differs in each nodule, making it nearly impossible to achieve continuous flaking. The irregular cortex adversely affects knapping. This flint is not useful for formal tool production.

Cortex condition

Limestone.

Cortex structure

Hard, rough, regular.

Cortex thickness

1 to 5 mm.

Cortex color

White.

Transition

The transition between flint and cortex is distinct, in some cases forming an even line, in other cases an irregular line.

Reddish-brown Bryozoan Flint

Name

The flint contains delimited zones of bryozoan fossils. Sample 43 was collected at Bjerge-by, NW Jutland, by Carl Johan Becker. Flint of both Danian and Senonian ages is present at this location. We have no further information about its provenience or this sample's geological age. Becker apparently classified it as Senonian, since he wrote "SEN" on the sample. Its glassy surface and structure place it closest to a Senonian flint, although we have no other examples of Senonian flint with this reddish-brown color. Samples 18 and 50 are collected in modern quarries and classified by the collector as being of Danian age.

Geological age

Uncertain. Both Senonian and Danian have been suggested.

Use of the flint

Not known.

Published references

Becker 1959.
Johansen 1987.
Thomsen 2000.
Vang Petersen 1993.

Geographical distribution pattern

Not known, but probably present in moraines in western Denmark.

Primary occurrence

Modern quarries at Thisted, Odby and Helligkilde, western Jutland, Denmark.

Secondary occurrence

Not known, probably present in moraines in western Denmark.

Present accessibility

Available at modern quarry sites.

Prehistoric accessibility

Sample 43 is collected at the site of the prehistoric flint mines excavated by Becker in 1959.

Location of reference samples

Sample 18, modern quarry at Odby, western Jutland, Denmark.
Sample 43, Bjerge-by, northwestern Jutland, Denmark.
Sample 50, modern quarry at Helligkilde, western Jutland, Denmark.

Flint color

Light reddish-brown with gray patches.

Flint structure

Fine  Coarse

Flaked surface

Smooth, slightly scalar.

Reflectivity

Shiny.

Homogeneity

Homogeneous structure. The flint contains some small bryozoan fossils in delimited zones and large gray inclusions up to 1 cm.

Translucency

Highly translucent.

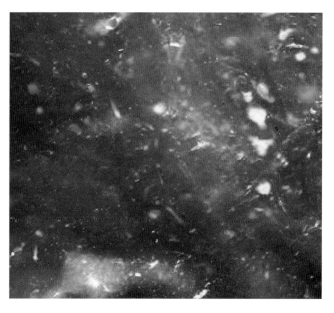

Nodule form and dimensions

Nodules are irregular. Size varies from fist-sized to 10 cm.

Other distinguishing characteristics

This flint is more fine-grained than most of the other bryozoan flints.

Knappability

Brittle  Tough

Very high quality flint, suitable for all kinds of knapping. The cortex does not affect knapping.

Cortex condition

Chalky.

Cortex structure

Soft, smooth, regular.

Cortex thickness

1 to 10 mm.

Cortex color

White.

Transition

The transition between flint and cortex is similar to what we observe on Gray Band Danian Flint: a zone of white flint with a distinct boundary just under the cortex.

Kinnekulle Flint

Name

Kinnekulle flint or Cambrian flint. This flint is the only Scandinavian flint which occurs solely in an area with primary deposits. Sw. *Kinnekulleflinta, kambrisk flinta.*

Geological age

Upper Cambrian.

Use of the flint

Mesolithic microblades, blades, small flake axes (Kindgren 1991). Schnittger (1920) notes a scraper of Kinnekulle flint in a Late Neolithic burial near Kinnekulle.

Published references

Carlsson 2004.

Johansson, *et al.* 1943.

Kindgren 1991.

Kinnunen, *et al.* 1985.

Königsson 1973.

Laufeld 1971.

Schnittger 1920.

Sivhed 2000.

Westergaard 1943.

Geographical distribution pattern

Kinnekulle in Sweden is the only known source.

Primary occurrence

Upper layers of alum-shale deposits at Kinnekulle, Sweden.

Secondary occurrence

Can be exposed by erosion in the area.

Prehistoric accessibility

Eroded out of primary deposits (Kindgren 1991).

Present accessibility

Quarry at Kinnekulle, Sweden.

Location of reference samples

Sample 11, alum-shale quarry at Kinnekulle in western Sweden.

Flint color

Speckled. The flint is basically dark gray overlain with shades of blue, green or brown.

Flint structure

Fine  Coarse

Flaked surface

Smooth, with an oily surface.

Reflectivity

Shiny.

Homogeneity

Homogeneous structure.

Translucency

Opaque.

Nodule form and dimensions

Nodules are angular and irregular. The largest nodules are up to 30 cm.

Other distinguishing characteristics

None.

Knappability

Brittle  Tough

This flint fractures not only conchoidally but also angularly and the numerous cracks in the nodules cause them to break apart during knapping. However, Kinnekulle flint is easily worked by pressure flaking and it is suitable for making microblades. The flint in the drier band under the cortex is unsuitable for knapping.

Cortex condition

Weathered.

Cortex structure

Hard, rough, irregular.

Cortex thickness

1 to 2 mm.

Cortex color

Brown or gray.

Transition

At the cortex and about 1 cm into the nodule the flint is coarser. Here it is matte and dry and lacking the oily appearance characteristic of the "fresher" material deeper in the nodule.

Ordovician Flint

Name

Sw. *Ordovisisk flinta; Öländsk flinta.*
Dk. *Ordovisisk flint.*

Geological age

Upper Ordovician.

Use of the flint

Microliths; known from settlements dating to the Boreal and early Atlantic periods on Öland, Sweden.

Published references

Alexandersson 2001.
Alexandersson, *et al.* 1996.
Kinnunen, *et al.* 1985.
Königsson 1973.
Laufeld 1971.
Tralau 1974.
Werner 1974.

14a–h

Geographical distribution pattern
The Swedish islands of Öland and Gotland, especially along the beaches but also in ploughed fields.

Primary occurrence
Upper Ordovician layers on the Baltic Sea floor.

Secondary occurrence
Beaches and ploughed fields on Öland and Gotland, Sweden.

Present accessibility
Beaches and ploughed fields on Öland and Gotland, Sweden.

Prehistoric accessibility
Beaches on Öland and Gotland, Sweden.

Location of reference samples
Sample 14a–h, SE Öland, Sweden.

Flint color

Because this flint is known only from secondary sources and it has been subject to weathering and patination, its original color is not known. The varieties we have collected show the following coloration:

a   Reddish-brown with blue flecks.
b   Red with flecks and white strings.
c   Gray with flecks and red strings.
d   Dirty white with faint beige bands and red flecks.
e   Gray or brown with a blue tinge and a dark blue band directly under the cortex.
f   Gray with numerous inclusions, flecks, and blue strings.
g   Milky white with tinges of blue or pink and pockets of darker strings which look like algae.
h   Gray with black flecks.

Flint structure

Variable.

Flaked surface

a   Smooth and glassy.
b   Smooth, slightly scalar.
c   Smooth, slightly scalar.
d   Smooth, slightly scalar.
e   Smooth and glassy, slightly scalar.
f   Smooth, slightly scalar.
g   Scalar.
h   Scalar.

Reflectivity

Varies from shiny to matte.

Homogeneity

Homogeneous structure.

Translucency

Varies from opaque to translucent.

Nodule form and dimensions

Nodules are usually rounded but some pieces are tabular. The largest nodules are up to 30 cm but these are generally of very poor quality and tend to break into chunks when force is applied.

Other distinguishing characteristics

The most distinctive characteristic of this flint is the oily appearance of a freshly flaked surface. The flint shows great variation. In many cases numerous fossils, rings, strings, etc. are visible in the flint. Occasionally the flint contains empty cavities.

Knappability

Knappability varies widely and the many fissures and cracks make the flint hard to work. The thin cortex has no effect on knapping.

Cortex condition

Limestone or weathered.

Cortex structure

Hard, rough, irregular.

Cortex thickness

1 to 10 mm.

Cortex color

a   Speckled black and white.
b   Yellowish-brown.
c   Yellowish-brown.
d   No cortex discernable.
e   White.
f   White.
g   Grayish-brown.
h   Yellowish-brown.

Transition

There is a sharp transition between flint and cortex.

West Swedish Beach Flint

Sample 12

Name

This category does not describe a homogeneous flint from a primary source but rather nodules of flint available on beaches along Sweden's west coast. Because they originate from several sources the nodules can also be of differing geological ages and appearance. Beach flint has also been observed along the south and southwestern coasts of Norway (Johansen 1956), see figure 25.

Sw. *Västsvensk strandflinta, kritflinta.*

Geological age

Variable ages.

Use of the flint

Flake axes, scrapers, drills.

Published references

Fredsjö 1953.
Johansen 1956.
Lidmar-Bergström & Johansson 1971.
Påsse 1992.
Werner 1967, 1974.

12

Geographical distribution pattern

Beaches and beach ridges on the Swedish west coast and from the coast to at most 50 km inland (Werner 1974). Also available on the southern coast of Norway (Johansen 1956).

Primary occurrence

Unknown.

Secondary occurrence

Beaches and beach ridges, moraine in western Sweden.

Present accessibility

Beaches and beach ridges, moraine in western Sweden.

Prehistoric accessibility

As above.

Location of reference samples

Sample 12, former beach ridge on the island of Hising, Gothenburg, Sweden.

Flint color

Gray, with pockets of chalk.

Flint structure

Fine  Coarse

Flaked surface

Scalar, somewhat gritty.

Reflectivity

Matte.

Homogeneity

Homogeneous structure containing pockets of chalk.

Translucency

Opaque.

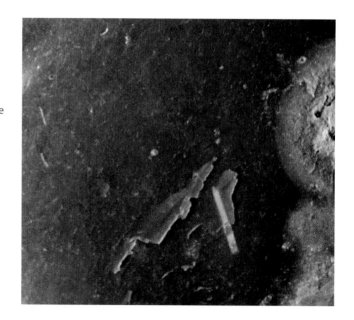

Nodule form and dimensions

Nodules are irregular. The largest nodules are 10 to 20 cm.

Other distinguishing characteristics

The flint contains concavities of chalk originating at the cortex and extending into the flint. In this respect it is similar to the type we call Matte Danian Flint, Östra Torp Variety.

Knappability

Brittle  Tough

Hard and tough. The chalk cavities and cracks in the flint prohibit good knapping control.

Cortex condition

Weathered.

Cortex structure

Hard, rough, irregular.

Cortex thickness

1 mm or less.

Cortex color

Yellowish-brown.

Transition

There is a sharp transition between flint and cortex.

Ball Flint

Samples 2 & 5

Name

This type encompasses secondary flint of varying ages and provenience. Characteristic is that the nodules have been subjected to heavy mechanical weathering by glacial ice and water. These actions have reduced them in size, ground them into spheres or oblongs, and removed most of their cortex.

Sw. *Rullflinta, kulflinta, bollflinta.*

Dk. *Kugleflint.*

Geological age

Variable ages.

Use of the flint

Microlith production in the Maglemose period, scrapers in the Neolithic.

Published references

Apel 2001.
Becker 1952b, 1990.
Knarrström 1997.
Königsson 1973.
Laufeld 1971.
Strömberg 1982.
Tralau 1974.

2, 5

Geographical distribution pattern
    Beaches on Bornholm, Denmark and southeastern Sweden.

Primary occurrence
    Unknown.

Secondary occurrence
    Beach deposits on Bornholm, Denmark and southern Sweden.

Present accessibility
    Beach deposits.

Prehistoric accessibility
    Beach deposits.

Location of reference samples
    Sample 2, beach on Bornholm, Denmark.
    Sample 5, beach on Bornholm, Denmark.

Flint color

Occurs in a variety of colors including gray, black, yellow, red and green.

Flint structure

Fine  Coarse

Flaked surface

Variable.

Reflectivity

Varies from shiny to matte.

Homogeneity

Homogeneous structure.

Translucency

Variable.

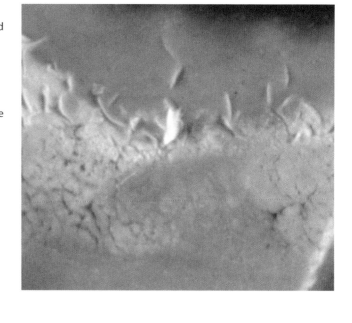

Nodule form and dimensions

The most characteristic aspects of ball flint nodules are their rounded or oblong shape and smooth surface. Nodules are generally small, usually less than 10 cm long.

Other distinguishing characteristics

None.

Knappability

Brittle   Tough

The hard and smooth outer surface makes direct percussion difficult, which is why this flint is usually opened using bipolar technique. The small size of the nodules limits the usefulness of the flint.

Cortex condition

Weathered.

Cortex structure

Not known, due to heavy weathering.

Cortex thickness

Absent or less than 1 mm.

Cortex color

Nodule surfaces can be white, black, gray or brown, depending on weathering conditions.

Transition

Variable.

We feel confident that *Scandinavian Flint* has convincingly illustrated the complexity of this raw material. As archaeologists we have long been dissatisfied with a classification into three types, Senonian, Danian and Kristianstad flint, and even Becker's classification into seven types has often proven to be inadequate. While three or even seven types is not sufficient for describing the variability of Scandinavian flint, opinions will differ as to how many types a satisfactory classification system should encompass. As with any such system, the aim is to capture the significant variation while at the same time keeping the number of types to a manageable number. Here we have proposed 17 types.

When we began this study, our ambition was to reach a level of knowledge whereby we could draw maps showing the primary and secondary occurrences of the various types of Scandinavian flint we defined. We soon discovered that complexity in the number, the location, and the character of the flint sources, both primary and secondary, makes such an aim impossible to realize. For this reason our maps show the location of our samples, but in support of the general picture we offer only verbal descriptions of primary and secondary locations. Now more than ever, we are suspicious of maps which purport to show the distribution of flint types in Scandinavia.

Due to the geological conditions here, with extensive flint transport caused by glacial and post-glacial activity, it is often difficult or impossible to identify the primary source of any particular piece of flint found in a secondary context. Patination also adds to our confusion, altering the appearance of flint after it has left its primary source. Our visits to flint sources have also brought home to us that flint from different places at the same locality can vary in appearance. For instance, it is widely known that layers of both Danian and Senonian age, containing flint of quite different appearance, outcrop at Stevns Klint. Perhaps less widely known is the fact that the Klintholm outcrop contains two flints of quite different appearance. Thomsen (2000:35) writes that the coarse bryozoan flint from Klintholm is the only kind of flint which can be provenienced with certainty. While it is true that flint containing the characteristic bryozoan fossils can be unequivocally identified as this type, the reverse is not true, however. That is to say, not all flint from the geological layers in which this flint occurs has this same, distinctive appearance. When visiting Klint-

Figure 63 Flint with the appearance of Scandinavian Senonian Flint is present in some layers at the quarry of Klintholm. This locality is the type site for Bryozoan Flint, Funen Variety, a flint of Danian age.

Bush, P. R. 1976. The use of trace elements in the archaeological classification of cherts. *Staringia* 3:47–48.

Bush, P. R. and G. de G. Sieveking 1986. Geochemistry and the provenance of flint axes. In *The scientific study of flint and chert,* edited by G. de G. Sieveking and M. B. Hart, pp. 135–140. Cambridge University Press, Cambridge.

Callahan, E. 1980. Report from Denmark. *Flintknapper's Exchange* 3(1):3.

Care, V. 1979. The production and distribution of mesolithic axes in southern England. *Proceedings of the Prehistoric Society* 45:93–102.

Carlie, A. (ed.) 2003. *Berättelser från Vætland. En arkeologisk resa längs E22 i Skåne.* Riksantikvarieämbetet & Regionmuseet i Kristianstad/Landsantikvarien i Skåne. Trelleborg.

Carlsson, T. 2004. Mellan kvarts och flinta. In *Mötesplats Motala – de första 8 000 åren,* edited by T. Carlsson, pp. 54–57. Riksantikvarieämbetet UV Öst, Linköping.

Carserud, L. 1994. *Geologiska sevärdheter i Skåne II.* Sveriges Geologiska Undersökning, Lund.

Cederschiöld, L. 1949. En yxa av kristianstadsflinta från Jylland. *Fornvännen* 44:53.

Cederschiöld, L. 1950. En håleggad yxa av kristianstadsflinta. *Fornvännen* 45:363–364.

Church, T. 1994. *Lithic Resource Studies: A Sourcebook for Archaeologists.* Special Publication Lithic Technology 3. Department of Anthropology, University of Tulsa, Tulsa.

Costopoulos, A. 2003. Prehistoric flint provenance in Finland: reanalysis of Southern data and initial results for the North. *Fennoscandia archaeologica* XX(2003):41–54.

Crabtree, D. 1967. Notes on Experiments in Flintknapping: 3. The flintknapper's raw materials. *Tebiwa* 10(1):8–24.

Craddock, P. T., M. R. Cowell, M. N. Leese and M. J. Hughes 1983. The trace element composition of polished flint axes as an indicator of source. *Archaeometry* 25(2):135–163.

de Bruin, M., P. J. M. Korthoven, C. C. Bakels and F. C. A. Groen 1972. The use of non-destructive activation analysis and pattern recognition in the study of flint artefacts. *Archaeometry* 14(1):55–63.

Ebbesen, K. C. 1980. Die Silex-Depots Südskandinaviens und ihre Verbreitung. In *5000 Jahre Feuersteinbergbau,* edited by G. Weisgerber, pp. 299–304. Deutsches Bergbau Museum, Bochum.

Ekström, G. 1936. Skånes moränområden. *Svensk Geografisk Årsbok* 12:70–77.

Floris, S. 1971. Fakse kalkbrud. In *Geologi på øerna. 1. Sydøstsjælland og Møn,* pp. 37–54. Varv, Copenhagen.

Floris, S. 1992. *Stevns Klints geologi.* Stevns Museum, Store Heddinge.

Francis, J.E. 1994. Fear and Loathing in Wyoming: Documentation and Evaluation of Lithic Procurement Sites. In *Lithic Resource Studies: A Sourcebook for Archaeologists,* edited by T. Church, pp. 230–234. Special Publication Lithic Technology 3. Department of Anthropology, University of Tulsa, Tulsa.

Fredsjö, A. 1953. *Studier i Västsveriges äldre stenålder.* Skrifter utgivna av arkeologiska museet i Göteborg. Nr. 1. Gothenburg.

Gang Rasmussen, T. 1999. *Sten på stranden.* Natur og Museum 38. Naturhistorisk museum, Århus.

Gardiner, J. 1990. Flint Procurement and Neolithic Axe Production on the South Downs: a re-assessment. *Oxford Journal of Archaeology* 9:119–140.

Gibbard, P. L. 1986. Flint gravels in the Quaternary of southeast England. In *The scientific study of flint and chert,* edited by G. de G. Sieveking and M. B. Hart, pp. 142–149. Cambridge University Press, Cambridge.

Glob, P. V. 1951. En flintsmedie på Fornæs. *Kuml* (1951):23–39.

Gry, H. and B. Søndergaard 1958. *Flintforekomster i Denmark.* Committee on Alkali Reactions in Concrete Progress Report D2. Danish National Institute of Building Research and the Academy of Technical Sciences, Copenhagen.

Hansen, F. 1929. Neolitiska "paleolitica". *Fornvännen* 24:247–249.

Henning, A. 1895. Spräcklig och enfärgad flinta i Sveriges mucronata-krita. *Geologiska Föreningens Förhandlingar* 17(1895):391–411.

Herrig, E. 1995. Die Kreide und das Pleistozän von Jasmund, Insel Rügen (Ostsee). In *Geologie des südlichen Ostseeraume – Umwelt und Untergrund,* pp. 91–113. Deutschen Geologischen Gesellschaft, Bonn.

Hewitt, H. D. 1915. Some experiments on patination. *Proceedings of the Prehistoric Society of East Anglia* 1915:45–51.

Holst, N. O. 1906. Flintgrufvor och flintgräfvare i Tullstorpstrakten. *Ymer* 1906(2):139–174.

Houmark-Nielsen, M. and K. H. Kjær 2003. Southwest Scandinavia, 40–15 kyr BP: palaeo-geography and environmental change. *Journal of Quaternary Science* 18(8):769–786.

Håkansson, E. and E. Thomsen 1999. Benthic extinction and recovery patterns at the K/T boundary in shallow water carbonates, Denmark. *Paleogeography, Palaeoclimatology, Palaeoecology* 154 (1999):67–85.

Hägg, R. 1954. Die Mollusken und Brachiopoden der schwedischen Kreide. Die Schreibkreide (Mucronatenkreide). *Geologiska Föreningens i Stockholm Förhandlingar* 76(3):391–418.

Høeg, P. 1994. *Fröken Smillas känsla för snö.* Norstedt, Stockholm.

Högberg, A. 1997. Flinta är flinta är flinta, eller…? *Bulletin för arkeologisk forskning i Sydsverige* 2(1997):34–42.

Högberg, A. 1999. Flintsmeder i Klagshamn – flinthuggningskonst och flinthuggare i början av 1900-talet. *Elbogen* 1998(65):181–192.

Högberg, A. 2001. *Öresundsförbindelsen. Flinta i yngre bronsålder och äldre järnålder.* Kultur Malmö. Malmö Heritage. Malmö.

Högberg, A. 2002. Production Sites on the Beach Ridge of Järavallen. Aspects on Tool Pre-forms, Action, Technology, Ritual and the Continuity of Place. *Current Swedish Archaeology* 10(2002):137–162.

Högberg, A. 2004. Flintavslag, åskviggar och eld – några aspekter på flinta i medeltid. *Elbogen* 2003(71):29–40.

Högberg, A. 2005. Hanaskog – en nyupptäckt produktionsplats för lövknivar. *Ale* (2005):1–6.

Högberg, A., J. Apel, K. Knutsson, D. Olausson and E. Rudebeck 2001. The Spread of Flint Axes and Daggers in Neolithic Scandinavia. *Památky Archeologické* 42(2):193–221.

Jansson, P. 1999. *Ängdalas gåta.* CD-thesis. University of Lund, Lund.

Johansen, E. 1956. Tilgangen på lokal flint i Øst-Norge under yngre steinalder. Et nytt syn på et gammelt problem. *Stavanger Museums Årbok* 1955:87–94.

Johansen, M. B. 1987. *Brachiopods from the Maastrichtian-Danian boundary sequence at Nye Klov, Jylland, Denmark.* Fossils and Strata 20. Oslo.

Johansson, S., N. Sundius and A. H. Westergård 1943. *Beskrivning till kartbladet Lidköping.* Sveriges Geologiska Undersökning, Ser. Aa 182. Sveriges Geologiska Undersökning, Stockholm.

Juel Jensen, H. 1993. *Flint tools and plant working. Hidden traces of stone age technology.* Aarhus University Press, Århus.

Kelly, A. R. and V. J. Hurst 1956. Patination and age relationship in south Georgia flint. *American Antiquity* 22(2):193–194.

Kempfner-Jørgensen, L. and D. Liversage 1985. Mere om Sejerøs forhistorie. *Fra Holbæk Amt* 1985:7–27.

Kindgren, H. 1991. Kambrisk flinta och etniska grupper i Västergötlands senmesolitikum. In *Västsvenska stenåldersstudier,* edited by H. Browall, P. Persson and K.-G. Sjögren, pp. 33–69. Ser C. GOTARC. Institute of archaeology, Gothenburg.

Kinnunen, K., R. Tynni, K. Hokkanen and J.-P. Taavitsainen 1985. *Flint raw materials of prehistoric Finland: rock types, surface textures and microfossils.* Geological Survey of Finland 334. Geologian tutkimuskeskus, Espoo.

Kjellmark, K. 1905. En stenåldersboplats i Järavallen. *Antikvarisk Tidskrift för Sverige* 17(3):1–144.

Kjellmark, K. 1939. Siretorpskomplexets fyndmaterial av flinta, sten, ben etc. (utom keramik). In *Stenåldersboplatserna vid Siretorp i Blekinge,* edited by A. Bagge and K. Kjellmark, pp. 71–102. Kungl. Vitterhets Historie och Antikvitets Akademien, Stockholm.

Knarrström, B. 1997. Neolitisk flintteknologi i ett skånskt randområde. In *Carpe Scanium. Axplock ur Skånes förflutna,* edited by P. Karsten, pp. 7–25. Arkeologiska undersökningar. Vol. 22. Riksantikvarieämbetet, Lund.

Knarrström, B. 2000a. *Flinta i sydvästra Skåne. En diakron studie av råmaterial, produktion och funktion med fokus på boplatsteknologi och metalltida flintutnyttjande.* Acta Archaeologica Lundensia 33. Almqvist & Wiksell International, Stockholm.

Knarrström, B. 2000b. Tidigneolitisk social och rituell organisation. Analys av 95 skivskrapor i ett depåfynd. In *Artefakter. Arkeologiska ting,* edited by A. Högberg, pp. 103–113. Report Series. Vol. 71. University of Lund, Lund.

Knarrström, B. 2001. *Flint a Scanian Hardware.* Riksantikvarieämbetet, Lund.

Knarrström, B. 2007. Boplatsaktiviteter belysta genom flintstudier. Råmaterial, teknologi och funktion. In *Vägar till Vaetland. En bronsåldersbygd i nordöstra Skåne 2300–500 f.Kr.,* edited by M. Artursson, pp. 97–106. Riksantikvarieämbetet och Regionmuseet Kristianstad, Stockholm.

Knutsson, K. 1988. *Making and using stone tools.* AUN 11. Societatis Archaeologica Upsaliensis, Uppsala.

Kragh, A. 1964. *Mand og flint.* Rhodos, Copenhagen.

Krüger, J. 1971. Kvartær. In *Geologi på øerne. 1. Sydøstsjælland og Møn,* pp. 61–93. Varv, Copenhagen.

Königsson, L.-K. 1973. Annan flinta. *TOR* 1972–73:48–52.

Laufeld, S. 1971. Geological age and provenance of some flint artifacts from Gotland. *Meddelanden från Lunds universitetets historiska museum* 1969–1970:96–98.

Lidmar-Bergström, K. 1982. *Pre-Quaternary Geomorphological Evolution in southern Fennoscandia.* Sveriges geologiska undersökning Serie C 785. Uppsala.

Lidmar-Bergström, K. 1983. Flint and Pre-Quaternary geomorphology in south Sweden and south-west England. In *The scientific study of flint and chert,* edited by G. de G. Sieveking and M.B. Hart, pp. 191–199. Cambridge University Press, Cambridge.

Lidmar-Bergström, K. and C. Johansson 1971. Flintfynd i södra Halland. *Svensk geografisk årsbok* 1971(47):62–72.

Luedtke, B. E. 1992. *An Archaeologist's Guide to Chert and Flint.* Archaeological Research Tools 7. Institute of Archaeology, University of California, Los Angeles.

Lundberg, T. 1976. Industrin i Grönhögen. In *Ventlinge – en sockenbeskrivning,* pp. 124–142. Ventlinge Hembygdsförening, Kalmar.

Madsen, B. 1984. Et forsøg med tilhuggning af Kristianstadflint. *Fjölnir* 3(1):77–90.

Madsen, B. 1993. Flint – udvinding, forarbejdning og distribution. In *Da Klinger i Muld… 25 års arkæologi i Danmark,* edited by S. Hvass and B. Storgaard, pp. 126–129. Aarhus University Press, Århus.

Madsen, B. 1994. Blegvad – et flintbrud fra bondestenalderen. *5 000 år under motorvejen.* Vejdirektoratet og Rigsantikvarens Arkæologiske Sekretariat, pp. 42–43. Vejdirektoratet, Copenhagen.

Magnusson, N. H., G. Lundqvist and G. Regnéll 1963. *Sveriges geologi.* Norstedts-Bonniers, Stockholm.

Malyk-Selivanova, N., G. Ashley, R. Gal, M. D. Glascock and H. Neff 1998. Geological-Geochemical Approach to "Sourcing" of Prehistoric Chert Artifacts, Northwestern Alaska. *Geoarchaeology* 13(7):673–708.

Matiskainen, H., A. Vuorinen and O. Burman 1989. The Provenance of Prehistoric Flint in Finland. In *Archaeometry: Proceedings of the 25th International Symposium,* edited by Y. Maniatis, pp. 625–643. Elsevier, London.

McDonnell, R. D., H. Kars and B. H. Jansen 1997. Petrography and Geochemistry of Flint from Six Neolithic Sources in Southern Limburg (The Netherlands) and Northern Belgium. In *Siliceous Rocks and Culture,* edited by A. Ramos-Millán and M. A. Bustillo, pp. 371–84. Universidad de Granada, Granada.

Micheelsen, H. 1966. The Structure of Dark Flint from Stevns, Denmark. *Meddelelser fra Dansk Geologisk Forening* 16:285–368.

Mjærum, A. 2004. *Å gi øksene liv. Et biografisk perspektiv på slipte flintøkser fra sørøstnorsk tidlig- og mellomneolitikum.* Hovedfagsoppgave i nordisk arkeologi, University of Oslo.

Nielsen, B. and E. Rudebeck 1991. Introduktion till arkeologi i Södra Sallerup. *Elbogen* 58:64–97.

Nielsen, F. O. S. 2001. Nyt om Maglemosekultur på Bornholm. In *Danmarks jægerstenalder – status og perspektiver,* edited by O.L. Jensen, S. A. Sørensen and K.M. Hansen, pp. 85–99. Hørsholm Egns Museum, Hørsholm.

Nielsen, L. E. 1993. *Proveniensundersøgelser af flint i europæisk arkæologi: metoder og muligheder – og muligheder i Danmark.* Hovedfagsspeciale. Aarhus university, Århus.

Nielsen, L. E. 1997. Raw material provenience in the early Neolithic. A comparative study of thinbutted flint axes from two regions in Jutland, Denmark. In *Man and Flint,* edited by R. Schild and Z. Sulgostowska, pp. 261–267. Institute of Archaeology and Ethnology, Polish Academy of Sciences, Warsaw.

Odell, G. 2000. Stone Tool Research at the End of the Millennium: Procurement and Technology. *Journal of Archaeological Research* 8(4):269–331.

Odell, G. 2004. *Lithic Analysis.* Kluwer Academic/Plenum Publishers, New York.

Påsse, T. 1992. Erratic flint along the Swedish west coast. *Geologiska Föreningens i Stockholm Förhandlingar* 14(3):271–278.

Påsse, T. 2004. Geologisk beskrivning av Falkenbergsområdet. In *Landskap i förändring. Hållplatser i det förgångna,* edited by L. Carlie, E. Ryberg, J. Streiffert and P. Wranning, pp. 25–42. Vol. 6. Hallands länsmuseer, Halmstad.

Randver, U. 2004. *Fynd av Flinta.* CD-thesis, University of Lund, Lund.

Rapp, G. J. 1985. The provenance of artifactual raw materials. In *Archaeological Geology,* edited by G. J. Rapp and J. A. Gifford, pp. 353–375. Yale University Press, New Haven.

Rasmussen, A. and C. Niss 2002. *Koralbanken – Faxe Kalkbrud.* Amtscentret, Næstved.

Rassmann, K. 2001. Vortrag zur Jahressitzung 2000 der Römisch-germanischen kommission. Die Nutzung baltischen Feuersteins an der Schwelle zur Bronzezeit – Krise oder Konjunktur der Feuersteinverarbeitung? *Bericht der Römisch-germanischen Kommission,* Band 81, 2000:5–36.

Rottländer, R. C. A. 1975. The formation of patina on flint. *Archaeometry* 17(1975):106–109.

Rottländer, R. C. A. 1989. *Verwitterungserscheinungen an Silices und Knochen.* Tübingen.

Rudebeck, E. 1981. *Ängdala. Flintgruvor från yngre stenåldern, S. Sallerup. Utgrävningar 1977 –81.* Rapport 1. Malmö Museer. Stadsantikvariska enheten, Malmö.

Rudebeck, E. 1987. Flintmining in Sweden during the Neolithic period: new evidence from the Kvarnby–S. Sallerup area. In *The human uses of flint and chert,* edited by G. de G. Sieveking and M. Newcomer, pp. 151–157. Cambridge University Press, Cambridge.

Rudebeck, E. 1994. Angdala och meningen med arkeologin. *Arkeologi i Sverige 3:/–40.*

Rudebeck, E. 1998. Flint Extraction, Axe Offering, and the Value of Cortex. In *Understanding the Neolithic of North-western Europe,* edited by M. Edmonds and C. Richards, pp. 312–327. Cruithne Press, Glasgow.

Rudebeck, E., D. Seitzer Olausson and U. Säfvestad 1980. Die südschwedischen Feuersteingruben – Ergebnisse und Probleme. In *5000 Jahre Feuersteinbergbau,* edited by G. Weisgerber, pp. 183–204. Deutsches Bergbau Museum, Bochum.

Salomonsson, B. 1971. Malmötraktens förhistoria. *Malmö stads historia* del 1. Malmö.

Schmalz, R. F. 1960. Flint and the Patination of Flint Artifacts. *Proceedings of the Prehistoric Society* 26:244–49.

Schmid, F. 1986. Flint stratigraphy and its relationship to archaeology. In *The scientific study of flint and chert,* edited by G. de G. Sieveking and M. B. Hart, pp. 1–5. Cambridge University Press, Cambridge.

Schnittger, B. 1920. Hälles och Kisas gravar på Kinnekulle. *Västergötlands Fornminnesförenings Tidskrift* 4(1):26–38.

Shockey, D.E. 1995. Some observations of polarization and fluorescence in primary and secondary source lithic materials. *Bulletin of the Oklahoma Anthropological Society* 44:91–115.

Sieveking, G. de G., P. Bush, J. Ferguson, P. T. Craddock, M. J. Hughes and M. R. Cowell 1972. Prehistoric flint mines and their identification as sources of raw material. *Archaeometry* 14(2):151–76.

Speakman, R. J. 2004. Unpublished report, available at the Department of Archaeology and Ancient History, Lund.

Speakman, R.J., H. Neff, M.D. Glascock and B.J. Higgins 2002. Characterization of archaeological materials by laser ablation – inductively coupled plasma – mass spectrometry. In *Archaeological Chemistry VI: Materials, Methods and Meaning,* edited by K. Jakes, pp. 48–63. American Chemical Society, Washington.

Stapert, D. 1976. Some natural surface modifications on flint in the Netherlands. *Palaeohistoria* 18:7–41.

Steinberg, J. M. and B. J. Pletka 1997. The value of flint in Thy, Denmark. In *Man and Flint,* edited by R. Schild and Z. Zulgostowska, pp. 301–311. Institute of Archaeology and Ethnology, Polish Academy of Sciences, Warsaw.

Strömberg, M. 1952. En privatägd fornsakssamling i Trolle-Ljungby socken. *Skånes Hembygdsförbunds Årsbok* 1952:84–98.

Strömberg, M. 1982. Specialized, Neolithic Flint Production. *Meddelanden från Lunds universitets historiska museum* 4(1981–82):48–64.

Surlyk, F. and E. Håkansson 1999. Maastrichtian and Danian strata in the southeastern part of the Danish Basin. In *Field Trip Guidebook,* edited by G. K. Pedersen and L. B. Clemmensen, pp. 29–68. Geological Institute, Copenhagen.

Thacker, P. T. and B. B. Ellwood 2002. The Magnetic Susceptibility of Cherts: Archaeological and Geochemical Implications of Source Variation. *Geoarchaeology* 17(5):465–82.

Thomsen, E. 2000. Flintens geologi og mineralogi. In *Flintstudier,* edited by B. V. Eriksen, pp. 17–36. Aarhus University Press, Århus.

Thorsberg, K. 1997. Den gropkeramiska kulturens o-väsen. In *Till Gunborg. Arkeologiska samtal,* edited by A. Åkerlund, S. Berg, J. Nordbladh and J. Taffinder, pp. 49–57. SAR. Vol. 33. University of Stockholm. Stockholm.

Thurston, D. R. 1978. Chert and flint. In *The Encyclopedia of Sedimentology,* edited by R. W. Fairbridge and J. Bourgeois, pp. 119–124. Vol. 6. Encyclopedia of Earth Sciences, Stroudsburg.

Tite, M. S. 1972. *Methods of Physical Examination in Archaeology.* Seminar Press, London.

Tralau, H. 1974. Micropalaeontological analysis of Ordovician flint artifacts from a stone age settlement at Ire, Gotland. In *Gotlands Mellanneolitiska Gravar,* edited by G. Janzon, pp. 247–249. Studies in North-European Archaeology 6, Stockholm.

Vang Petersen, P. 1993. *Flint fra Danmarks Oldtid.* Høst & Søns Forlag, Copenhagen.

Vang Petersen, P. 2001. Grisby – en fangstboplads fra Ertebølletid på Bornholm. In *Danmarks jægerstenalder – status og perspektiver,* edited by O.L. Jensen, S.A. Sörensen and K.M. Hansen, pp. 161–174. Hørsholm Egns Museum, Hørsholm.

Vemming Hansen, P. and B. Madsen 1983. Flint Axe Manufacture in the Neolithic. An Experimental Investigation of a Flint Axe Manufacturing Site at Hastrup Vænget, East Zealand. *Journal of Danish Archaeology* 2:43–59.

Weisgerber, G. 1980. Fornæs bei Sangstrup, Gem. Hammelev, Jütland. In *5000 Jahre Feuersteinbergbau,* edited by G. Weisgerber, pp. 470–472. Deutsches Bergbau Museum, Bochum.

Werner, M. 1967. Flintfynd efter svenska västkusten. *Ymer* 1967:227–242.

Werner, M. 1974. *Flintförekomsterna på svenska västkusten.* PhD. University of Gothenburg, Gothenburg.

Westergaard, A. H. 1943. Den kambro-siluriska lagerserien. In *Beskrivning till kartbladet Lidköping.* 182 Ser. Aa. Sveriges geologiska undersökning.

Wienberg Rasmussen, H. 1970. *Danmarks geologi.* Jul. Gjellerups Forlag A-S, Copenhagen.

Wienberg Rasmussen, H. 1984. Blottede lag fra Danmarks undergrund. In *Landskabernes opståen,* edited by A. Nørrevang and J. Lundø, pp. 131–160. Danmarks natur. Vol. 1. Gad natur forum, Copenhagen.

Williams-Thorpe, O., D. Aldiss, I. J. Rigby and R. S. Thorpe 1999. Geochemical Provenancing of Igneous Glacial Erratics from Southern Britain, and Implications for Prehistoric Stone Implement Distributions. *Geoarchaeology* 14(3):209–46.

Wray, D. 2005. Test report 092. Analytical Unit, University of Greenwich. Available at the Department of Archaeology and Ancient History, Lund.

Wyszomirska, B. 1988. Flint Production and Flint Trade in Northeastern Scania. In *Trade and Exchange in Prehistory,* edited by B. Hårdh, L. Larsson, D. Olausson and R. Petré, pp. 83–98. Acta Archaeologica Lundensia, Lund.

Personal communication

Kärrefors, D. 2001. Personal communication.

Sivhed, U. 2000. Personal communication.

Thorsen, M. S. 2003. Personal communication.

Wray, D. 2006. Personal communication.

Internet sources

"Fakse Kalkbrud" http://www.aabne-samlinger.dk/oestsjaellands/kalkbrud.htm

"FlintSource.net" http://flintsource.net